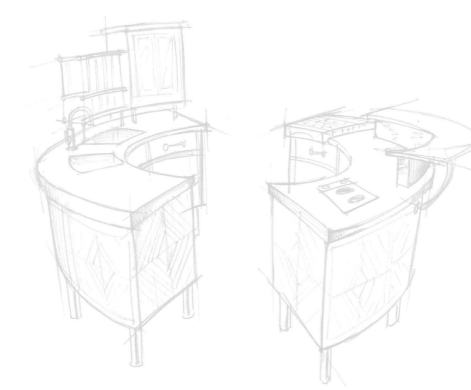

kitchen culture

Johnny Grey

kitchen culture
reinventing kitchen design

location photography by Alex Wilson

FIREFLY BOOKS

A FIREFLY BOOK

Published by Firefly Books Ltd. 2004

Text copyright © Johnny Grey 2004
Photography, design and illustration
copyright © Jacqui Small 2004

First printed in Great Britain in 2004 by
Jacqui Small, an imprint of Aurum Press Ltd.

First printing

Publisher Cataloging-in-Publication Data
(U.S.) available upon request.

Library and Archives Canada Cataloguing in
Publication data available upon request.

Published in the United States in 2004 by
Firefly Books (U.S.) Inc.
P.O. Box 1338, Ellicott Station
Buffalo, New York 14205

Published in Canada in 2004 by
Firefly Books Ltd.
66 Leek Crescent
Richmond Hill, Ontario L4B 1H1

Printed and bound in China

This book is dedicated to all the wonderful women who have given me inspiration, kindness and loyalty. The list includes special friends, clients, and those who have enriched my life as well as those who have worked for me. To Becca my wonderful wife, Guss my daughter, Christabel my late, gentle sister, Diana my loving mother, Anna my recent loyal business manager, Lucy my artist and sister-in-law, Libby my mother in law, Vidya my complementary doctor, Peg my US CEO, Charlotte, Jill, and Sarah, the talented teachers of all my children at Dunannie school, and my young nieces who represent the future – Katherine, Carmody, Rose and Sienna.

contents

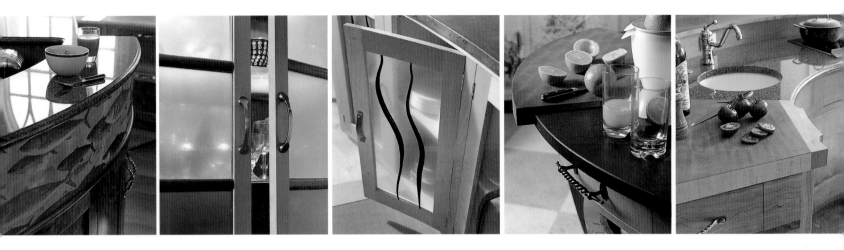

foreword by Alice Waters

I am grateful to Johnny Grey. Not long ago he came to my restaurant, Chez Panisse, in Berkeley, California, stayed for lunch, and charmed me with tales of his aunt, Elizabeth David, whose books changed my life. How delightful that her nephew is now a celebrated kitchen designer and the author of this useful book. In the 60s, when I was a poor student living in London, I all but stalked Elizabeth David, devouring her books, hanging out at her shop, fantasizing about what her own kitchen must look like, hoping to catch a glimpse of her but too shy to introduce myself.

Elizabeth David's aesthetics inspired every detail of Chez Panisse, which I wanted to feel like someone's home, not like a restaurant. Instead of multiple choices, I offered our guests one meal only, *table d'hôte*. Instead of hiding the kitchen behind tufted leather swinging doors, we built an open hearth and tore down the wall between the kitchen and the dining room, so diners would see their dinner cooking on an open fire. Instead of stainless steel everywhere, we chose butcher block and copper. We didn't want Chez Panisse to have the look of shiny efficiency.

It is important to remember, as Johnny Grey does, that the real purpose of kitchen design is not so much to maximize functionality and easy cleanability as it is to inspire deep delight and purest pleasure. As he writes in these pages, it all begins with light. In my own home kitchen, it took me over two years to figure out how to light the long oval table that seats 12 and sits in front of the big brick fireplace where I do most of my cooking. There had to be good light on the workspaces, but without that eye-level glare you see in gleaming "professional" kitchens. There had to be overhead light at the table, so you could see what you were eating, but there also had to be light from below, disappearing into the dark-beamed ceiling above and creating that magical zone of warmth around the table. I would have solved this problem faster with Johnny's help!

For me, the ideal kitchen has to include a zone of hospitality. There must always be room for the rest of the family and unexpected guests, and the space should invite everyone to help out. It should be high-ceilinged and low-tech, filled with objects and tools that make you feel good and that feel better the more you use them. There should be a big table, comfortable chairs and doors that open onto a kitchen garden. All the utensils, dishes and glasses should be exactly where you expect to find them. There has to be a large walk-in pantry, a big working fireplace and preferably an antique stone sink, but the details are less important than the object of designing a room where you can live every day, a room that inspires your creativity, your craft and, above all, your generosity. Thanks to Johnny Grey for offering us this perceptive guidebook to a praiseworthy ideal.

introduction

I am fascinated with the idea of the kitchen, what it means and how it is changing. I am an architect by background, a kitchen designer in practice and I work on kitchens around the world. This book is set around the projects I have done and the ideas associated with comfortable living – in well-designed environments. It is about how the way we live in our houses is changing; the kitchen now seems to be in the process of slowly occupying the whole downstairs floor space.

The dynamic behind our use and understanding of kitchen space has altered. For some the kitchen is now becoming an open-plan multipurpose space; for others its new role is partly disguised. I believe the design of most houses in the future will be planned around a thoroughly different version of the kitchen as we know it today. It will have an effect on the way the whole house will be used, radically changing the name, size and function of the main floor of the home. These observations are based on current social, economic, cultural and lifestyle trends that are available for us all to see in people's homes, in articles and through the way we are constantly adapting to contemporary life. Living patterns change so much faster than bricks and mortar. This book explores how redefining the design of the house opens up huge opportunities for a new sociable, active central space with room for several different activities to be played out simultaneously. It will be welcoming, bright, efficiently planned, comfortable and heart-warming – with more freedom to move around. However, we still need careful design for culinary activities, and much of the advice in this book, on subjects like cooking ergonomics, apply equally well to our current kitchen spaces.

We need to think imaginatively about what a kitchen is for us individually. We need to explore the story around it, examine its history, its contemporary meaning, its possible future and, most importantly, its design potential. This book is a design manual at heart, and it appeals to thinking differently about how you imagine a kitchen. Its design needs to succeed on so many counts, from ergonomics through to layout, from lighting to the pleasure of using it. If you don't enjoy being in the space, you won't linger or have an inclination to use it.

Most new homeowners want to install their own kitchen as soon as they move in – reflecting personal views and the latest in interior design concepts or fashions. However, the issues are larger than they may appear. Today hardly a single house in the U.S. or Europe has the right space to accommodate the new expectations for the kitchen, in terms of size, location or relationship to the other rooms and the outside.

When you have finished remodeling your kitchen space and are enjoying your first proverbial sip of wine, remember as you look across the room, scanning its textures, shapes and colors, that it all started with an idea. It always surprises me how much power ideas have and how important it is to have a strong vision and stick with it. So when you are going through the sometimes tough, awkward, or trying moments on the way there, keep this moment in mind. It will be worth it. I hope this book makes it a more exciting and successful task. A great kitchen is at the heart of every happy family and every contented soul.

Johnny

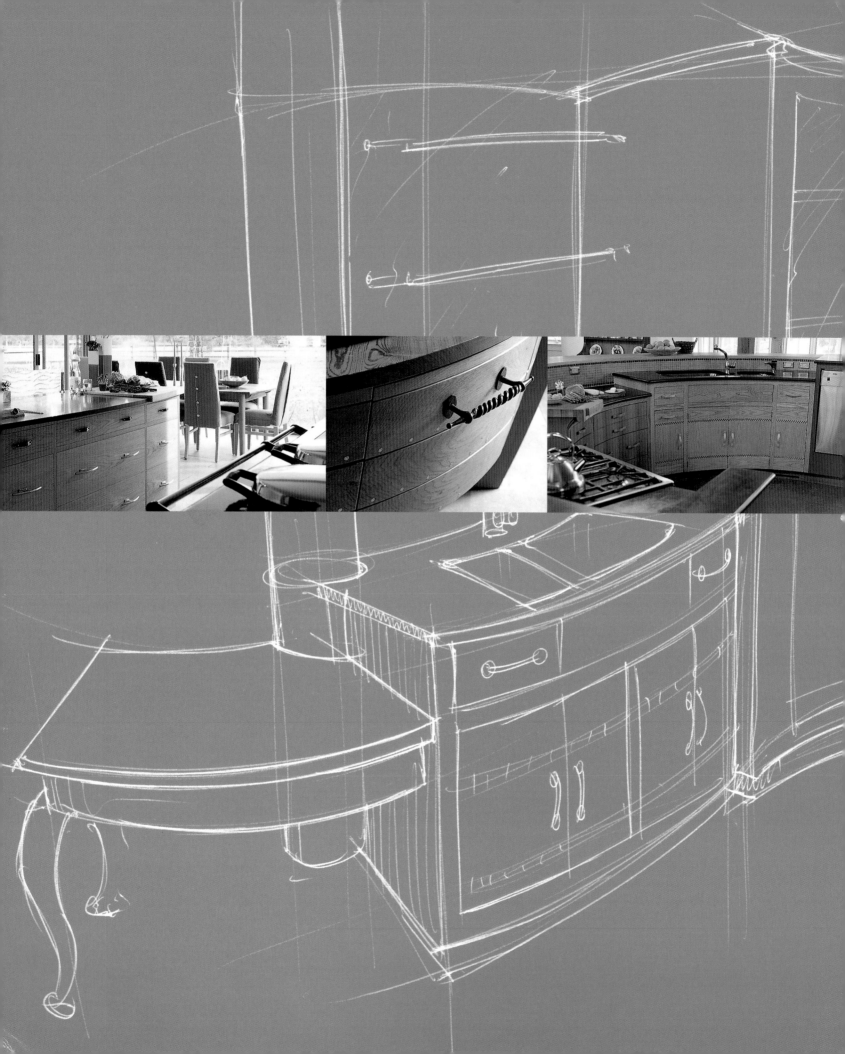

kitchen culture: reinventing home space

In 1987 when Ruthie and I opened the River Café, we wanted the kitchen to be visible. Our first kitchen was designed so that the customers had to walk through the kitchen to enter the restaurant. The kitchen was the first act in the drama. When we designed our own kitchens at home, we put our kitchens in the middle of the living area, too. You have the pleasure of cooking while being able to talk to your guests this way, and are able to get people involved with the food preparation, and teach them about what you are doing. The greatest pleasure for me is being able to share what I am doing, and share my knowledge of cooking while I am doing it, whether it be with my children and grandchildren at home, or with the customers at the River Café.

Rose Gray
and Ruth Rogers

a fresh home perspective

History holds on to house design. Bricks and mortar are solid, heavy and not easily moved. House designs are affairs of the head; ethereal, changeable notions that remain free-floating in the world of ideas. Ideas are fast, plentiful and disposable; they liberate us from the everyday and rescue us from dull environments. Yet once executed, we face conundrum again – the built world holds us to ransom with a long timeline. Change is slow and cumbersome in physical terms.

ABOVE The new kitchen has become the active zone of the house, with an emphasis on sociability. Individual needs can be built into alcoves or accommodated within screens, thereby defining activity areas such as children's play areas, home work places or places in which to relax in comfort.

While we live differently from our parents and grandparents, we live mainly within their walls. To dig ourselves out of this inherited design history is hard, sometimes expensive. Remodeling rather than rebuilding is an exciting challenge, but the truth is that the design of our houses would need to be completely reconsidered to fully accommodate a lot of the ideas I am proposing in this introduction.

What is so key about kitchen design? It is the word "kitchen" itself that leaves us short. There is general agreement that the kitchen is the essence of home, a substitute for the hearth. The kitchen has become the new hallway. A cup of coffee or tea, which we consider more of a greeting than hospitality, means you go to the kitchen first, whether you are a service engineer or a dear friend who has traveled miles. Active home life orbits around it as we spend so little time together as families with such an increase in leisure pursuits. Social life conjures up friends coming in, family moving between rooms, pets coming and going and visitors dropping by to conduct the business of life. Traditionally, activity was diverted into public rooms such as a dining room or living room, but this behavior is becoming extinct. Rooms in today's houses have few restricted zones, and the kitchen is becoming the active multipurpose space choice as we go beyond the era of small rooms and segregated activities. This concept should allow us to realize how to reorientate our homes to a lifestyle that suits us better.

We live less formally in almost every sense. We dress more casually, eat with much less ritual and treat each other with more familiarity. The disintegration of the class system (in most cultures) plays a welcome part in the more relaxed house design for the middle classes. There is no segregation of servant's quarters, and children by and large don't have separate areas. We use our houses in a different way. With computers and electronic media becoming wireless and portable to an ever greater extent, and with the blurring of boundaries between private conversation in public, what will be truly private anymore? In addition, by blurring the boundaries further with open-plan multipurpose living spaces, it seems the rule book on privacy is being rewritten. We need it less or in different ways. We have a real problem with sound privacy, in particular from loud TVs, music systems, road traffic and outside noise, and yet we still need to be able to withdraw in moments of sadness or when exhaustion touches us. Whatever else is deducible from all this change, it is that large open-plan spaces accommodate the cross-pollination of family activity so much better than small or private family rooms.

ABOVE A new kind of kitchen is emerging that has little to do with the old apart from having cooking facilities. Homeowners choose their spatial needs – originally defined as "rooms" – and amalgamate them into one ground-floor space.

the starting point for change
Our forebears with their newly discovered need for privacy embarked on a course of separating functions in the early nineteenth century. Apart from the increasing belief that being genteel was to make most body functions discreet, the need for warmth in northern climates and those with harsh winters justified small rooms.

The starting point for liberating us from historical living patterns is to look at both past and present role models and fresh sources of visual inspiration that can give us a new ground map to remodel our home environments. There is now no real gap between "downstairs" home life and the kitchen – it's just a giant mood board for displacement activity, provision of zones for activities and their different requirements. All we need in addition are some highly serviced areas for bathing and soundproofed areas for noise making, media indulgence and sleeping – and maybe a garden or a terrace and a nearby gathering place to meet friends, too.

the experience of space

ABOVE The kitchen can be an adapted or mixed version of any "room" you want, not just through additional functional pieces of furniture but also through special alcoves, ambience, decor or simply through regular personal use as a flexible space. The only ingredients absolutely necessary are enough space and the willingness to carry out your ideas.

The new kitchen space is very flexible. The room that used to be for culinary activity is now a place where anything goes, awaiting designation. For my aunt Elizabeth David it was in reality a study where she wrote cookbooks. Table space, surfaces aplenty to put research papers on, culinary equipment to enable her to carry out recipes of a specific nature and also for books awaiting consultation, a *chaise longue* for reclining on and, finally, a modest space for display of seasonal produce, china and assorted favored objects. For a friend of mine from the West Country in England, the kitchen was her living room, she had no other. There is a semblance of relaxed comfort attached to a slightly shambolic room full of non-matching sofas, handmade rugs and piles of books, magazines and toys. For a jeweler friend in California the kitchen was more akin to a workshop. Jewelry construction is slow, thoughtful and relatively clean work. For an amateur publisher in Kent, England, our project was to construct more of a library than a kitchen, so we built in bookshelves aplenty. For an art collector client in Lake Tahoe it is a gallery with space for pictures. Colors of the furniture, walls and work surfaces must be considered carefully. The kitchen is a great opportunity for displaying furniture and paintings. You have permanent viewing attendance for the paintings, and in between, the furniture gives the kitchen use and three-dimensional enclosure. The walls are effectively a blank canvas for artistic expression yet with a functional edge.

interior revolution One of the most desirable lifestyle images we hold in our minds today might include New York lofts, generous open spaces overlooking the city, filled with light and combined with a cool, modern aesthetic waft into our imagination. We are, as a generation, intolerant of the lack of sunlight. We want as much light as possible, everywhere, albeit under control for filtering and for minimizing heat reduction or for privacy screening. Bigger spaces with more windows mean sunlight penetrates farther into the heart of the living space. Light travels more easily across open spaces, giving one a greater sense of freedom. In northern climates rooms were traditionally planned around heat sources. This is no longer the case. Central heating has been around for several generations so it is clear that we no longer need a house to be a series of small rooms. Small rooms segregate activity, are inflexible, often dark and waste space on corridors. Big spaces create more ease and sociability; they enable you to accommodate more activities within sight of each other. This means better communication and an opportunity for a more accomplished kitchen design.

The new sociable kitchen has been described as being like a medieval great hall where use was merely occupation or anything that was required of household life, sleeping included. The open plan is the modern version of this and sprang from the Arts

The drama of home life is played out in the kitchen. We commune, hang out, watch TV, telephone friends and relations, read the paper, do homework and hobbies, lounge on the sofa, cook and entertain, play music, argue and make up – all in one space.

and Crafts tradition of using hallways as living spaces. Frank Lloyd Wright expanded the hall as an idea across the house, and with the new availability of metal beams, large spans of wall-less space could be achieved without too much cost.

Staircases in the kitchen are one of the best ways of getting more pedestrian traffic into the space as well as bringing the upstairs corridors and circulation into the equation. The whole house starts to become easier to circulate in and feels more integrated. This makes us think in terms of "Kitchen Central."

The big changes we are seeking are a reaction to being dissatisfied with conventional home organization. One activity per room as an idea of organizing home life will start to disappear and, along with it, the constraints of poor use of space and isolation.

Increasingly in Britain, northern Europe and North America there is a need to try to reverse the trend for families eating out of sync with each other. In some cases, families eat less than one meal a week together. A shared meal is not just a ritual, but also a vital tool for communication and nurturing in a family. New open-plan multipurpose family kitchen spaces allow families to spend more time together and engage in better communication. The design ideas throughout this book also recognize the importance of the table as a key sociable part of the space (see Planning for Sociability, page 176). In addition, the process of cooking is carried out in full view and at the physical and emotional center of the home. By eating together, one heightens a shared interest in food, the practice of cooking with care and the value placed on family sociability.

ABOVE Calling the new space "Kitchen Central," like a railroad station, rather than an end destination such as "living room kitchen," is more helpful. One new feature is the inclusion of a staircase so that it becomes a circulation artery with access to other rooms, taking over some of the functions of a hallway.

food and foreign influences

It is perhaps stating the obvious to say that food affects the atmosphere of the kitchen. It does, but not in the way you might think. Quiet and effective kitchen machinery like fridges and dishwashers, central heating, more space, good extraction systems – these all make more of an impact on the way a kitchen is designed than the native cuisine of the household. The cultural traditions we impose upon the raw ingredients and family rituals associated with its consumption are also more significant than the method of preparation in the way we use kitchens. Our eating habits are the greatest driving forces for change. As outlined in *The Rituals of Dinner* by Margaret Visser. Visser outlines the fascinating number of rules, equipment, decoration, sequencing, bodily positions and codes of behavior surrounding the consumption of food. From biological necessity to becoming a culturally controlled phenomena, how we eat food is no accident. The design of the environment around eating has to accommodate these food-associated social mores.

During the week the use of fresh, semiprepared meals increasingly account for the vast majority of "home cooked" meals. In contrast, cooking "from scratch" can't be achieved everyday if you have a busy lifestyle or career. It is an efficient use of resources and an understandable compromise to buy pre-prepared food, and as long as it is fresh with good ingredients it is not that much different from going out to eat, and we certainly don't need to feel guilty about that.

For most of us, true home cooking is done at weekends. You not only need time to cook but also to shop. A lot of menu choice is done by eye feasting or visual stimulation. The ultimate way to buy food is at the market where dazzling displays inform you on what is in season and you are stimulated into a decision in the most desirable way through mountains of plump red tomatoes and shiny purple eggplant.

If you follow food writers such as Alice Waters, or Rose Gray and Ruth Rogers at London's River Café, they all emphasize the importance of respecting growers and producers of food, of using farmers' markets and organically grown ingredients. Cooking from scratch is a hard task for the time-deprived during the week, but on weekends is popular whether as a hobby, for sheer pleasure, or as an expression of love – or all three.

food traveling During the weekend when I have time to relax a little and speculate about the week that has passed, I express my desire for mental release, to be somewhere else, to travel, through the cooking of some evocative dish. From plain to highly exotic, light to rich, it does not matter – but it must be foreign. Depending on my mood it can be seasonal or merely whimsical. What we want to recreate in our home kitchen environments is different from previous generations. We may not wish to recreate the Museum of Modern Art at home, but by having an Eames chair or pottery from Provence, we can enjoy a memory of our vacations and to a wider cultural milieu.

Reading a cookbook is a form of food traveling. Judging by the plethora of cookbooks available as well as the number of programs on TV and the sheer quantity of food-based articles in the newspapers and magazines, the anticipation of food is as marketable as the act of eating. Indulgence is as much in the contemplation as eating. Books written by good food writers speak so eloquently of food culture and bring diversity and practical ways to reinvoke foreign elements into one's life. This mirrors the role of the kitchen rather appropriately. The kitchen is not just for cooking a series of well-balanced recipes – it is for bringing in a whole mental landscape from other places, other times and other geographies.

We snack almost as much as we dine now. Not every meal is a major refueling exercise. We like cafés, bistros and metropolitan bars because they feed us fast and lightly and because they uplift us from the confines of our ordinary day jobs. They

ABOVE AND OPPOSITE Cooking for pleasure and relaxation through recipes from other cultures takes us on a journey to foreign places, stirring memories and evoking exotic associations. It helps us reinvent ourselves and enhances the pleasure of living.

Your craving for food is accommodated by instinct. Seasonal produce, and the healthy variation it creates in our diets, prompts us to use more effort to cook well and with variety in a way that reading about it in a book or article cannot.

provide a brief escape to a friendly environment. The classic ingredients for a good time are there – food, spirited company, drinks – all set within an evocative décor. The most accessible places of public hospitality are the cafés where you can wander casually off the street and relax for a few minutes of welcoming revival. A serious sit-down meal is a pleasure, but it requires time and usually is a planned destination. Cafés engage us in temporary ready-to-go conversations, transient snatches of friendly discourse. Not all conversation needs a long meal to make it enjoyable. The local café remains the hospitality ancestor of the roadside inn. Weary feet and refueling stops for humans, they can be the easiest of places to congregate, especially in a warm climate where the activity of the street provides an outside focus of pleasurable interest. Agreeable places to hang out – restaurants, cafés, covered markets – affect our identification with a neighborhood. Environment intercepts our moods. In design terms, a place to perch or sit with a temporary or peripatetic quality seems as necessary as a dining table in the new sociable kitchen.

reliving café culture at home
After a hard day at the office, it is sociability as much as food that is in demand. The sharing of a drink (the aperitif of hospitality) does not require the accompaniment of large amounts of food, but more a titillation of different spicy flavors, a quenching of appetites. A glass of wine with traditional Spanish tapas or Lebanese mezze offers a civilized companionship to easy flowing conversation. Local flavor gives an authenticity and purpose closely linked to the idea of family hospitality where the décor is individual and the expression of the family identity part of the experience. Cafés have an air of easy sociability. Relaxed and yet with a prompt pace when required, they reflect many of the current paradigms of home life practiced in the new kitchen – food on demand, a quixotic menu and a continual flow of people. With the right ingredients, home life can reflect these sociable qualities. The future kitchen should reflect the new enjoyment of the tapas culture – that longer experience of the pre-meal or lighter snack that offers flavor over quantity within a sociable milieu.

leisure together
Families want to spend the precious home-time together between being at work or school that takes such a large chunk of our day. Expanded leisure activities and vacations take us out of home too. If work has expanded in hours, out-of-home leisure has also grown. With many households having two working partners the pressure on family time together is even greater. I believe this is one of the greatest pressures for working toward "one space for active living, with kitchen included." We want to spend what time there is in visual contact and not be isolated in a separate room two hallways away.

OPPOSITE Many parallels exist between conscienscious design of contemporary café interiors and the home kitchen: an environment of easy sociability in which flexible menus are served.

psychology of kitchen culture

Psychologists use the term "mental maps" to explain how we process large amounts of information and arrange it in patterns to file it in ways that we can retrieve. The way we fertilize change is through applying these maps – acquired from multiple sources – into a specific project – for example, a kitchen or an interior design space.

We are a society increasingly sophisticated in interpreting visual images. Advertisers purposefully leave gaps in commercials to allow the viewers to perceive themselves cool because they "get" it. We accumulate visual references in huge quantities. The average interior design magazine has at least 2,000 items to digest. From billboards to TV, newspapers and the internet, it has been calculated that we can touch base with 10,000 images a week. We file away these visual "hits" and act on them later when we might want to change or improve the way we want to live. From the idea of downsizing to changing our aesthetic identity, we can switch from being a traditionalist to a lover of contemporary chic. Do we like change or do we want to play safe by being conservative? I believe we secretly formulate many of these visual "hits" as mini experiences. They have an attached emotional impact – however small the "hit." We are probably not aware of how they are changing us. Our sensibilities are being altered subliminally and over a period of time. They inform us how we want to live. The kind of messages prevalent today with regard to home interiors are clearly sending new messages about what defines our idea of what being at home means. A redefining of home is taking place.

Escapism is a common desire, and one way it expresses itself is the need for calm. In design terms, Oriental-style interiors and the associations of Zen or Buddhist practices bring easy access to a meditative state. This partly explains the popularity of minimalism. It is a normal desire to want to retreat into a safe place at times. Nesting does not mean just escaping, it implies comfort and renewal. The classic request from our clients is for a couch in the kitchen, an area for children to play next to their parents and the more feminine application of color and styles of furniture, and access to a garden.

ABOVE An experience shared: food is the sociable adhesive for modern living, and with it comes a plethora of cultural references, all of which can be explored within the domestic kitchen from preparing ingredients to the gathering of family and good friends.

signifier of culture
Upgrading your status through the new kitchen? For some this is a route to being cool or being one up on the neighbors. We can enhance our status and enjoy the advantage of good design at the same time. The kitchen is a major part of the value of a house, and although I do not share the slightly cynical approach, it needs acknowledging. When status takes over and we do not listen to our intuitive needs, then redoing a kitchen becomes driven by the wrong motivations.

LEFT The kitchen should be furnished like any other room in the house. Its culinary efficiency can be disguised within the furniture. Dedicated work areas based on sound ergonomics come into their own when cooking starts.

In an article in the *Independent* newspaper, Stephen Bayley, leading design commentator, wrote that the kitchen is now an all-purpose middle-class entertainment zone, the signifier of culture. "Kitchens are literally laboratories of taste, the places people experiment with style, demonstrate their sophistication, flash their wealth."

Once upon a time, it was the car outside that made the major statement of who you were and your success. The kitchen has acquired new status. The man has now got a firm foothold inside the door. The kitchen is no longer the preserve of an enslaved woman in the house. It is now an equal opportunity employer. Kitchens are decided by couples jointly – and each with their own ideals in mind. The result of this is that the purchasing power of kitchens is greater, the spaces are bigger and the traditional male-oriented appliances (technology-based products and gadgets), services and music systems are bigger, more complex and prestigious. The Cadillac outside has come indoors to the kitchen.

Appliances as tools or as status symbols? They are both. Large fridges, ranges, dishwasher drawers, wok burners, massive air extractors – there is increasingly more demand for the top-end manufacturers to make status symbols for those with the desire for something different and well made.

appliances as icons

Identifiable icons are the unchanging products of a kitchen – the appliances. Today's kitchen leaders include Sub-Zero fridges, Viking ranges, equipment from La Cornue, or Gaggenau. Fifty years ago, appliances dominated the kitchen industry. Post-war ads of dream kitchens featured refrigerator-freezers with some paltry cabinetry. Today the opposite applies. Apart from the prestigious large appliances mentioned above, appliances are formulated to submerge into the sizing of the kitchen cabinets. In relatively mundane "look-like-next-door" kitchens, only these appliance icons stand out as beacons of quality in an industry that has been ruled by ever-decreasing price, as quality is a now a major issue where demand is dominated by price. The beacon appliances stand to gain added status as a result.

What to buy in order to gain that reassurance that you have bought something good proves that the brand matters. Brands, the big bad boys of a consumer society that is concerned with antiglobalization issues, come to the rescue as visible icons but throttle creativity in kitchen cabinetry design. Style over substance, or at least over thinking about how to make the kitchen work as a holistic expression of good design, is a dead end street. Individual statement is often the only way of producing a satisfactory result.

bodily comfort

We all have images, dreams and fantasies of what our ideal comfortable home might feel like. I believe that to define being truly "comfortable" we could add ergonomically correct body support together with an element of luxury.

The two strands of comfort – the psychological aspect and the body support – need satisfying. It is not good enough to make a stylish kitchen without consideration for ergonomics. Equally, the cold comfort provided by laboratory-like efficiency with no psychological warmth, pattern or "craggy edges," is poor design. They both need each other and are judged by different criteria. Bodily comfort and the idea of moving with a sense of economy – which has the added advantage of efficiency of body use and time – is something I learned from the Alexander Technique.

Protection of our backs is also important to our sense of security, especially when we are sitting down. You may notice how in restaurants the tables around the walls fill up first. Looking into the center of the room is always preferable when cooking or prepping. Having activity going on behind you feels uncomfortable. A clear view of people coming into the room is also important. Relaxing in or near a walk-through area is unsettling. If a view of the entrance area into your house is possible from the kitchen, particularly from what I call a key or "driving position," for example, between the island and the sink, assuming the cooktop range is in front of you, this is a real bonus for receiving visitors.

a role for design One of the main justifications of being a designer is to make the physical environment comfortable. That means making the dimensions of the things we interact with fit human dimensions. There is an increasing demand for a well serviced environment. Underfloor heating, limestone floors, sophisticated lighting, natural high-performance materials and attractive décor are part of what many individuals have come to expect.

Ergonomics is essentially the study of efficiency and how designers plan for easy use. To get into a tub, the sides need to be not too tall and the floor not too low or slippery; to use a work surface, the counter has to be adjusted in height for what we are doing, and be appropriate, hard-wearing material. The kitchen benefits from someone who knows and cares about these technical requirements and can make them work in harmony. Anthropometrics, the study of human measurement, is a valuable tool to apply for making the user fit with what is being used. Kitchens are spaces where you can benefit hugely from careful planning because the pressure of using the space is great in terms of its potential performance and the durability of materials over a long time. Bodily comfort is achieved through using high-quality materials, good design thinking and careful execution. Custom building and original design work is the best way of achieving this.

ABOVE Ergonomics may form the basics of comfort, but without the backup of wider psychological aspects, such as feelings of warmth or something pleasing to the eye, then why linger in a kitchen space? The tactile qualities of natural materials, the enchantment of natural light on color and the use of pattern assist.

influencing design

Social life outside the home is different in every culture just like our forms of salutation. Climate, historical traditions and built environment affect what form social life outside the home takes. The equivalent of the village square, the Italian hillside town piazza, the souk or bazaar in the Middle Eastern, the marketplace in French towns and the many urban meeting places draw us away from our homes into a social opportunity of both expected and unplanned meetings. How we use our kitchens is affected by this now that they are social spaces. Metaphorically speaking, the kitchen is the domestic version of the village square. A cousin I spoke to about how I design kitchens observed that what I was essentially doing was designing for social relations. This may sound farfetched, but a successful home is underpinned by lots of real conversation and human contact.

ABOVE Kitchen culture depends on a foundation of serious study in how to support the body in anthropometrical terms and making the space work in practical ways.

bringing the outside in In cities the increasing regularity of dining out affects our vision of the kitchen. It makes it less a place for cooking and focuses more on sociability, sitting around chatting, snacking, reading or simply hanging out. We mimic a little of our experience of cafés, gastro pubs, diners or sushi bars, even fast food outlets into our home interiors by a process of mental proxy. Being out is stimulating and sociable, and it offers sustenance without demanding any effort. Being in is the better alternative after you have been exhausted by travel or work.

The design of bars, restaurants, and boutique hotels is a useful inspiration and source of design ideas for the new sociable kitchen. They are useful because a skilled designer has taken the essence of hospitality, played with its dramatic elements from lighting through to color, theme, and manipulation of space and turned it into an operational space. Commercial dining establishments need clever design to maximize use, atmosphere and excitement. The growing body of professionals who design restaurants and hotels have much that homeowners and kitchen designers can learn from. They are turning theater into three dimensions. Homes may not be stage sets exactly, but without an element of drama and style our interiors can be dull places.

Designing for social relations: as with a favored café or restaurant, a successful house is underpinned by lots of real conversation and human contact.

boutique hotels – home reinvented

Boutique hotels offer real and imagined experience. With time short on trips away they can provide a taste of home away from home but with added fantasy. They offer a relaxing atmosphere and a chance to get away from the boredom of airports and staying with international hotel chains. We crave revival of the spirits to relieve the stress experienced in today's hectic traveling schedules.

Books on hip hotels have become bestsellers. Their descriptions of these inviting places of great style and originality make you want to indulge in the whole experience. From Rome to Miami you can blend into an interior and take on not just a temporary persona while you are there but memorize the atmosphere. Relaxing and being pampered in spas, soaking up the atmosphere of inspiring décor and sampling exotic menus all combine to influence how you want to live at home, even if it is an unrealistic dream.

design gratification

The relevance of all this is confirmed when you realize that designers are trying to mimic the experience of being at home as part of the core rationale of their design for restaurant environments. The institutional limitations of a hotel are transcended by reenacting domestic comforts and a use of theatrical techniques. Emotional gratification through the décor as well as the service of the staff is key. Generous use of sumptuous materials like glass, contrasting materials and fabrics, wooden floors, lighting design, dramatic details and rich ornament make you luxuriate in the chosen mood. Collections of antiques from furniture through to objet d'art, modern art collections of paintings, lithographs to sculptures, themes which are linked to the architecture, invented heritage like a well-off aristocratic family – all provide the cocooning in an imaginary world of beauty and surreal experience that lifts you away from the everyday world. The only missing ingredient is that one has full service, while at home you have to do it yourself!

ABOVE Attention to detail in a restaurant or cafe, whether simple or grandiose, is a critical benchmark in terms of conveying the overall hospitality of an establishment. The domestic kitchen can be viewed in much the same way in view of its design.

authenticity Desire for real experience is a deep need in a society where we have commercial exploitation of almost all acts of consumerism. The search for authenticity to make the space yours, as opposed to a trend borrowed from a magazine, is a personal journey in which you discover your taste and response to immediate surroundings. Respecting the fabric of the building, maximizing natural light, views, removing corridors, enhancing the architecture through good quality floors and lighting, is a matter of judgment and skill. Authentic interiors must avoid the use of one style, plurality being a key to authenticity. It is an appreciation of the timeless way of doing things by furnishing a space in a relaxed way; a collection of beautiful, practical things, personal favorites and family heirlooms. Obsession with current trends leads to a kitchen that looks dated within a few years. Using freestanding old or hand-made pieces of furniture, and natural or recycled materials, can counteract this. Carrying out some of the practical work yourself helps connect one with the whole process, and is

BELOW As with the design of the most modern and chic bar interiors, the kitchen needs to be planned to complement the architectural context and reflect the artistic sensibilities of its users.

invaluable as a way of understanding the work and effort that craftspeople, builders and professionals put into home remodeling.

The search for authenticity is partly about creating a sense of place while being emotionally intelligent about choices. How does one seek the heart of a design, making something real and individual? In his ground breaking book *Authenticity*, David Boyle makes a checklist on what constitutes being "real." It includes being truthful, being simple or traditional in one's habits, and being connected to locality where appropriate; using humane processes in the way an item is made, not using a factory-made version, particularly if it is a mass-produced copy of a traditional or hand-made item.

In close sympathy with what Boyle describes as the New Realists is Morris Berman in his brilliant indictment of contemporary life, *The Twilight of American Culture*. The antidote to resisting "a new dark age whereby the commercial ways always rule" is by choosing to live by authentic values. Actions are taken like in medieval monasteries for their intrinsic benevolence, or capacity to improve the health of society and our

Interior decoration is about colors, textures and "the look." Design's primary task is to make the whole environment work. Measurement, body movement, light, space – these are the core matters of design.

environment. He proposes developing authentic skills. This might sounds farfetched in relation to the world of interiors, but is not the kitchen one of the best places to start? Less reliance on fashion and more on methods of execution, and expression of ourselves as authentic personalities, can create a greater sense of comfort and durability.

design and hospitality Hospitality is orchestrated at a

commercial scale through the use of intelligent design decisions. Sometimes the décor is just a light backdrop, and its elegance allows the food and people to do the work of making the ambience. At others it's heavily loaded with a theme that can substitute for the presence and direction of a real proprietor. This is so often what makes a restaurant a success. Immediately interesting and hard-to-measure qualities have to be catered to such as emotional issues like how welcoming the place is and what customers will find attractive. Is it to be an intimate place for young people or to be a good dining experience for those who want to get away from the everyday? At what social group will it be aimed and what will they find attractive? It is like having to give permanent dinner parties to people you don't know and catering for numbers you cannot predict. The design of domestic kitchens is helped by analyzing how you wish to entertain and receive visitors.

I recently designed a restaurant in London, England, for Foxtrot Oscar where the aim was to create good-value comfort food to be enjoyed within an appropriate marine environment. We chose a Nantucket fishing café as our inspiration. Recycled worn and distressed floors alternating with linoleum for the high-traffic areas, whitewashed brick walls, a suspended ceiling fashioned out of a sailcloth, handmade metal balustrading and a simple oak bar with a pewter top made a friendly and slightly rustic escape from everyday London life. The finished effect was intimate, but without trying to merely produce a domestic space; the materials, combined with the overall design brought a relaxed environment flexible enough to appeal to families, older couples and young people coming in groups.

the kitchen of the future

We are often stuck in preconceived ways of thinking about our home décor and living habits. However, by studying the possible future developments that may affect how we live – from social habits, environmental changes, and new technology, we can be sure of dramatic change.

In the future we may have rooms with transparent walls. Where will we put the furniture? With space defined by activity, culinary preparation circles will need genuine furniture, not wall-based cabinets. Furniture will be like sculpture. Freestanding pieces of no name may double up food display units or seats; counters for preparing food may be shaped around the human body; mobile screens may allow various degrees of exposure and functional use which will be both the location for downstairs activity and provider of transparent corridors. The unfitted kitchen, a term I invented in the mid-1980s for a kitchen conceived as a series of pieces of freestanding furniture is now entering into a new phase with its sculptural edge. You can't describe a kitchen space as a sculpture collection, but free-form, bio-form furniture gives a few clues as to how new furniture might look when production will allow it. Certainly buildings such as the Guggenheim Museum at Balboa are leading the way in architecture. Functional sculpture sounds a bit pretentious, but we need to loosen up our obsession with straight lines and rectangular shapes. They limit design possibility and the chance for a softer, more humane way of planning domestic spaces.

Working from home is a traditional and yet modern habit. It increases the time available for more productive work other than commuting, but it also makes for a potential hermitlike existence. Loneliness can be an issue – not enough outside input and sociable exchange. An attic room for home work is fine for when you need to concentrate, but for some low level concentration tasks, it is good to have a desk in

the kitchen or when members of the family are out and the house is quiet, personally I like to be in the kitchen, especially if there is a great view or an empty sun-trapped table handy.

Whatever else is clear the office as we have known it seems on the verge of transition? Susan Greenfield in her book *Tomorrow's People* looks at how technology is changing the way we think and feel. She talks about the beehive mentality of humans "surfacing as an increasingly important factor – the need to feel part of a busy, thriving community." At home, the active living space kitchen replacement is a good place to be to compensate for hours spent doing home "work."

Imagine for a moment arriving home, 2020. Step into the distribution port, glance through your head-up display – a perfect overlay of information and images on the "real" world – settle into the realm of household life. Peter Kingsley, a highly respected futures

futures expert, has been working on this area with me. We have been speculating on the future of home space. Our vision is for the kitchen, hallway, living room, and dining room to emerge as a single flexible space that re-shapes itself on demand. Peter believes that the new space "will incorporate a media zone that immerses you with global news and entertainment through a new form of video realism, augmented now with touch and smell. Voice commands turn on the oven, fade the lights and with barely a thought you hook deep inside the Grid, the pervasive and invisible post-web utility." We no longer believe kitchens will be kitchens, more like one space for active living, with kitchen included.

Kitchen environments are not just counters against walls. They need to be humane places that reflect our personalities and respond to future needs and technological changes.

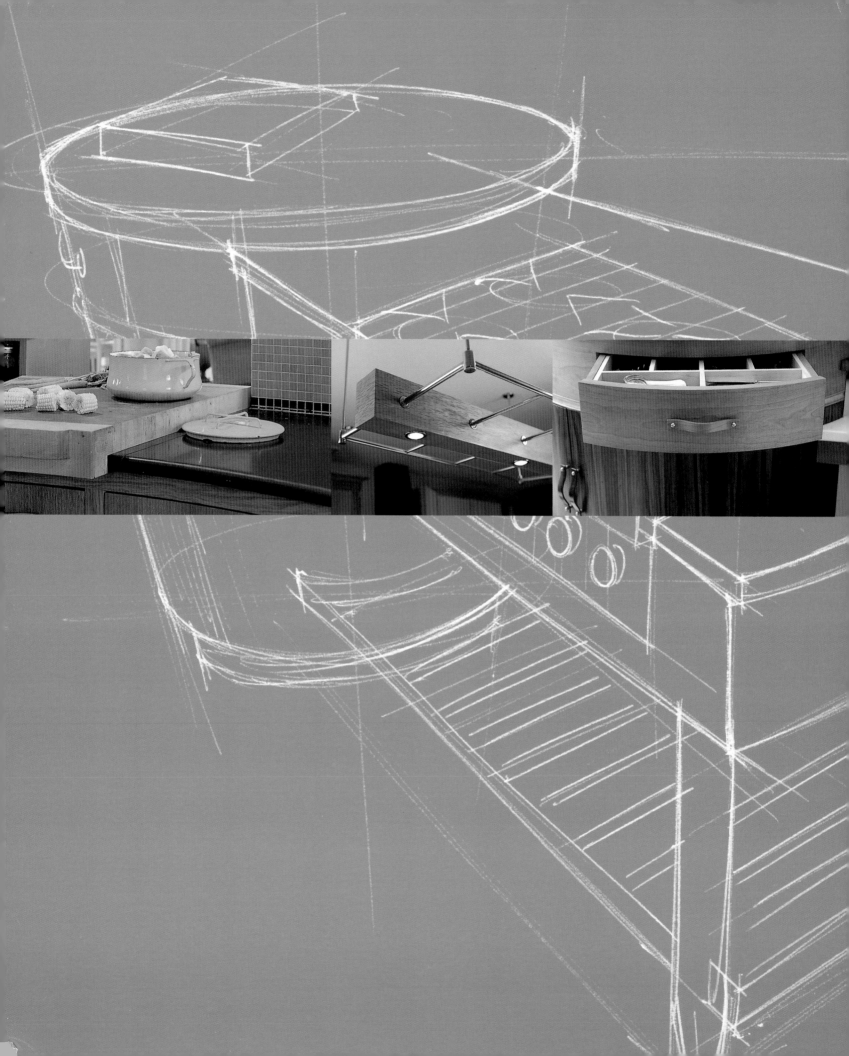

the core
of kitchen design

Much basic living is done in the space we call the kitchen, but much thinking time takes place there, too. Our nesting instincts are expressed in widely differing architectural envelopes, making each experience of designing a kitchen a unique challenge. This section shows eight projects with key concepts highlighted – from soft geometry to the use of natural light – that sets up the possibilities for a comfortable kitchen life.

The kitchen is essentially a collection of ideas set around a word. It could be defined in terms of great ideas mingling with furniture and furnace; objects of utility mixing with those of desire and style; a place of comfort and friendly architecture, or numerous conversations enjoyed over lovingly prepared meals. The opportunity for such richness can provide a greater sense of possibility. This first section of the book paves the way for you to expand your idea of what a kitchen can be.

good use of light

a design objective that brings well-being and enchantment

RIGHT The arc that the sun makes inside a room lays down its own hierarchy, a kind of priority furnishing footprint – especially in rooms that are deep or where windows are confined to one elevation. In this glass box design there is no conflict with the original architectural style, resulting in a calm, neutral addition to the internal space that brings a sense of the garden indoors, giving the kitchen maximum exposure to daylight.

It dances and shimmers and offers us direction in which to work, relax or eat. The less we have it, the more we crave its benediction. Initial conversations about kitchen design begin with light, and planning is dominated by it. How to maximize its effect is a design challenge like no other as we bathe in light for well-being. Think of Impressionist paintings by Monet or Renoir, which literally dance with light and recall how the effects seem both enchanting and ethereal and how much you want to be in them.

There is rarely enough natural light in interior spaces. Only so many rooms in a house can face south (or north in a southern climate). As humans we are like butterflies in that we are activated by sunlight; its ethereal presence washes us with contentment. The arc that the sun makes inside a room lays down its own order, especially in rooms that are deep or recessed, or where windows are confined to one elevation. Human-centered design should therefore start with selecting the best opportunities for light.

A false wall built to hide unreachable corner space uses the recess to create an alcove, housing a plate rack above the sink cabinet.

The curved sink cabinet works as a parallel curve to the central island making movement easy and directional. The user has peripheral sightlines that are wider because it is farther from the walls, and the body is in smoother motion to the left and right. It also creates an excellent working relationship with cooking and preparation facilities.

Appliance garage and a back-up work surface taper in shape to allow easy access to entrance doors into the kitchen. This geometry line is also related to the shape and position of the cooking area on the island.

Low-level area that feels more like a table is deep enough to sit at because of the distance from the cooking area. A Larva stone surface on a stainless steel frame makes the structure robust enough to be used for rolling out pastry or kneading bread.

Giant custom-made three-part armoire comprised of a pair of cupboards flanking a fridge made from squares of aspen veneers and maple frames that alternate directions.

Freestanding china cabinet with built-in parallel dishwasher drawers at an ergonomically pleasing height. The upper level glazed section is set back as the china is best stored within easy reach.

Circular preparation area can be approached and used from any angle. End grain block, used as ideal chopping surface, is sandwiched between flat grain oil-finished maple.

When considering the layout in this kitchen in south London, England, we speculated upon building a central island that would be defined by sun coverage or a table positioned to absorb the sun's reach either at breakfast or lunchtime. Could it be positioned to stay in sunlight all day in a northern climate? Was it worth considering the position of the sun in the winter rather than the summer Solstice on the basis that we are more starved of sun in winter than summer? The only problem with this was that this room had no direct sunlight! Throughout the day the sun creates its own moving dynamic, but it would be outside in the garden or at the back of the kitchen in the hallway. There was an answer waiting for us.

Homeowners Simon and Jeanette felt they had a shortage of space and light. The orientation of the house had almost no southern aspect. A small amount of direct sunlight came in through the hallway. Their underutilized asset was the charming but small outside garden. Simon was motivated by a new business idea of "building extensions" that were effectively glass boxes, comprising neutral-in-style glazed structures that could work anywhere and with any historical building style. Their kitchen would be a prototype for his new business of creating glass extensions to suit any home.

The addition of this glass structure was primarily to achieve more floor space and increase the light levels, but a bonus would be to alter the quality and intensity of the incoming natural light. The first decision was to use a limestone floor to help bounce the reflected light up and around into the room, particularly at the back where there was less. The tone and color of the stone chosen for the floor tiles is calming, being neither too white nor overly reflective and with plenty of variation in the grain. The use of brushed stainless steel on the main island structure and canopy with its neutral, but cool tone created an opportunity for playful elements of bright color to be used – in the dishwasher, china storage cabinet and alcove behind the sink – without creating design overkill. The texture of the stone work surfaces adds subtle variation and allows the sweetness of the cabinetry woods used – a mixture of elm and sycamore with accent panels of London Plain and Mazur birch – to make a subtle visual effect. The balance of stone with wood, of paint with stainless steel or glass, offers a myriad of couplings. Surfaces and texture play a notable role in this modern minimalist design because the lack of detail gives them more

prominence. The overall effect is one of contemporary calm with warm tones.

Interestingly, the glass box takes away the conventional boundary of windows and opens up the room, and those who occupy it, to the garden in an extreme way. The light level in the kitchen is very high, which makes it appear more spacious than it is, and the impact of changing weather is more acute. As evening approaches, a whole new opportunity is offered since there is a natural switch to focus upon the outside space through the glass box. The garden is artificially lit with pockets of light, creating dramatic effects with the shapes of plants, shrubs and structures of the trees. Shadows and dark voids appear and bring with them depth and privacy, as well as the mystery of the night. Daylight has its limitations because

ABOVE The furniture is orchestrated as a series of separate pieces but part of one composition. The freedom of expression allows for each item of furniture to have its own character, but keep a relationship with its neighbor and a sense of direction so they complement each other.

LEFT The use of soft geometry to create a kitchen facing into the light called for unorthodox, nonsymmetrical geometry – a series of self-contained pieces that each fulfill the criteria of dedicated work areas. The different shapes and sizes of the furniture makes for an unexpected but pleasing sense of movement, in both a practical and an aesthetic way.

ABOVE There is no hard and fast rule about all pieces having to be free-standing. The sink cabinet linked as a work surface, is needed here and a gap would be frustrating. The curved shape is satisfying to use as it wraps around the body and directs it in a relaxing way.

of lack of control and its ubiquitous evenness. The dramatic effects of artificial light can be utilized to great effect in determining atmosphere and mood. As the garden is effectively part of the interior landscape, its lighting becomes part of the interior lighting scheme, too.

We felt the need to aid the calming effects of this well-lit space by minimizing the hard geometry that is apparent in so much kitchen design. Too much cabinetry, jutting out peninsulas and hard corners make a harsh impact on easy movement. If there is nothing sharp near us, our peripheral vision need not work as hard; our self-defenses become inactive and we relax more. It is not surprising that small rooms are no longer popular, especially in spaces where there is a lot of movement, in a kitchen, for instance. Small rooms suit winter activities where you are in a more

defensive mode, and may fulfill single pursuit activities like watching TV or reading, but where there is going to be movement, we need space.

The layout of Simon and Jeanette's kitchen is planned around an island with a circular end and a short linear path set at an angle that responds to the easiest flow through the room. This provides a maximum work surface. The curved sink cabinet works as a parallel curve to make movement easy, and it is clearly directional. The corner is built out to minimize the feeling of being trapped, and an alcove is taken out of the false wall to house a plate rack.

As there is plenty of natural light here, the planning of light is driven by priorities that are less hierarchical and more democratic. Light washes throughout the space, and the free-standing furniture pieces benefit – they have independence and the space around them is not cramped. The new sociable kitchen has more of a summer aspect to it with its abundance of light and feelings of openness to the outside. We need reminders of summer in a northern climate to survive the exigencies of sun deprivation. That we need constant subliminal hints of summer in our kitchen life is no surprise. And with that, the glass extension surely helps and may do the same for many others in the future.

RIGHT As this room is so open to the garden, the colors, shapes and materials all seek to blend in, rather than confront. Sky-blue walls and the pale green in the dishwasher cabinet reflect garden sensibilities. The limestone flooring finds its way to the outer terrace beyond. Overall, the soft geometry creates more natural boundaries.

changing the parameters of a kitchen

an all-in-one, multipurpose kitchen and living space

In city apartments where there is little space available for more than a large cupboard or where only culinary preparation is aimed for, then we clearly read the space as a working kitchen. For most family houses and bigger apartments, we need a new umbrella term that incorporates the word "kitchen" but allows room for an expanded meaning to describe its newly acquired role. Rooms change use without necessarily changing name. For example, in an 18th century house, the word library meant a place for quiet study and reading of books; however, a century later, it described a family room with a scattering of books, more akin to a modern-day den. The Victorians had grand ideas, and "living room" or "parlor" would have been too lowly a description.

Kitchens have been expanding in the amount of space they occupy in most households over the last 20 years or so. Statistics vary, but in the U.S. it has increased by 45 percent, yet the amount of space we use for culinary activity has not.

Do we need kitchens anymore? There were rumors that new houses and apartments were being built in Seattle and Florida without kitchens – with just microwaves and tiny sinks in a cupboard. Will we adapt to houses without kitchens in the way that we have adapted to rooms

OPPOSITE In traditional Southern houses, kitchens were separate buildings from the main property. In this newly built kitchen space, it has become more like a barn with the structural beams dominating the roof. Yet it feels airy and comfortable, and provides a setting for a very modern idea – the all-in-one multi-purpose kitchen.

ABOVE A large space gives you the freedom to move around, and the design can therefore be generous with space. By combining key culinary activities with well-proportioned kitchen furniture and incorporating them within a circular counter, a cooking circle offers a practical solution to the expansive area and a view into the center of the room for good sociability.

without fireplaces? In urban centers where there are plenty of restaurants and cafés it is perfectly natural that the role of the kitchen is diminished, especially since the contemporary focus is on the quality of socializing and gathering in spaces other than the domestic framework. However, changing lifestyles and planning of homes make the role of the modern kitchen very important, but it should be seen not as a separate space or destination but a fluid, melted-down hallway – a cross between the medieval idea of one-room living and a more modern version – that of a quietly unassuming, amorphous home space, wherein the kitchen may be partly hidden within furniture and architecture and intermingle with the social functions of this new, central, daytime activity space.

One of my first questions when seeing new clients is to ask them if we are really planning a kitchen. After the first look of surprise, they usually get what I am saying rather

quickly and immediately become excited. Animated discussion then begins and with it a sense of liberation, sparking lots of new thoughts and discussion points:

- Do we need a wall to enclose the staircase if we want to encourage circulation?
- Where can we find extra space?
- Can we absorb another room and amalgamate it into this new "kitchen central"?
- Do we want a fireplace with a soft seating area focused around it?
- Where (if at all) does a TV go?
- What kind of flooring finishes are appropriate now that the space is larger – especially as stone is cold in large quantities?
- If the space is heated by radiators, do we want to use up valuable wall space for them? Underfloor heating is an option, but it not suitable with wooden floors

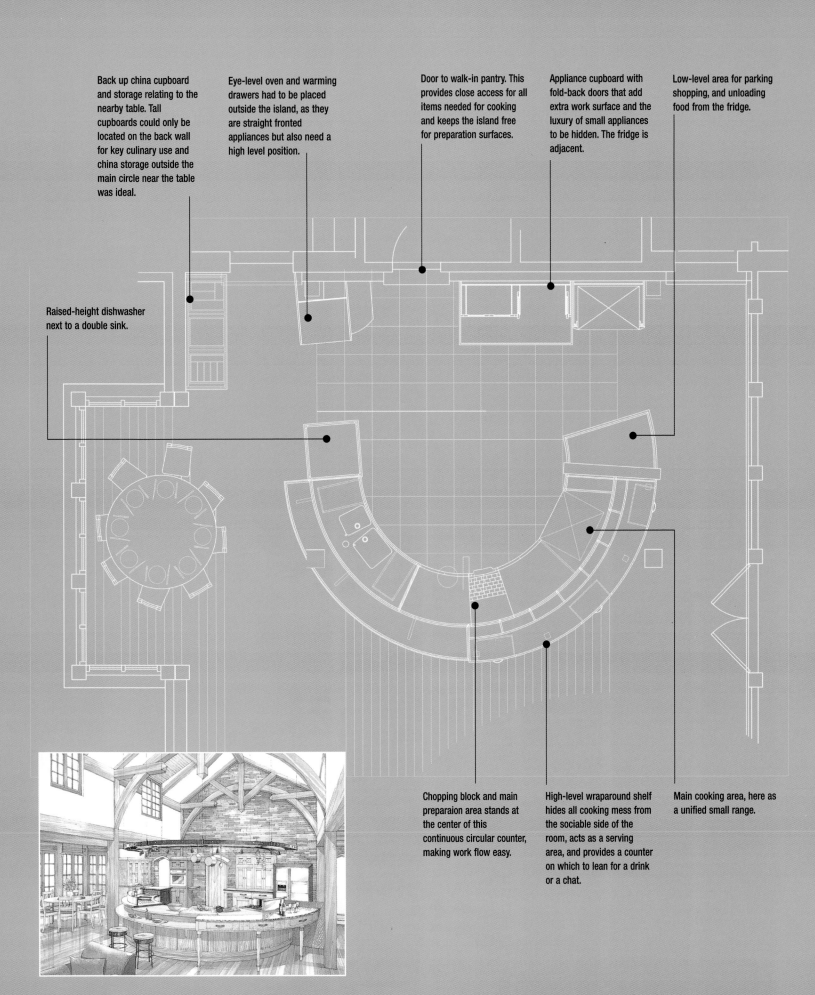

Back up china cupboard and storage relating to the nearby table. Tall cupboards could only be located on the back wall for key culinary use and china storage outside the main circle near the table was ideal.

Eye-level oven and warming drawers had to be placed outside the island, as they are straight fronted appliances but also need a high level position.

Door to walk-in pantry. This provides close access for all items needed for cooking and keeps the island free for preparation surfaces.

Appliance cupboard with fold-back doors that add extra work surface and the luxury of small appliances to be hidden. The fridge is adjacent.

Low-level area for parking shopping, and unloading food from the fridge.

Raised-height dishwasher next to a double sink.

Chopping block and main preparaion area stands at the center of this continuous circular counter, making work flow easy.

High-level wraparound shelf hides all cooking mess from the sociable side of the room, acts as a serving area, and provides a counter on which to lean for a drink or a chat.

Main cooking area, here as a unified small range.

In this kitchen in a newly built house in Memphis, we discussed a lot of these issues. The main part of the house was to be built along classic traditional American Colonial lines. "Comfortable and familiar" was the request. The kitchen was more of a challenge. In response to a changing way of living, the clients wanted to enjoy a lot of family time together.

The architects involved had not had the experience of designing large sociable kitchens where the distances were great and wall space limited. We spent some time deliberating over the size, layout and design of the whole space, which became a wing of the house rather than its core. This gave us plenty of freedom to have a separate aesthetic sensibility. Slowly it dawned on us that we were creating a barn rather than a domestic room.

The shape of the curved island was inspired by the need to enclose the culinary area. Its design reflects the idea of an open cooking area in a modern restaurant where the chefs are considered performance artists rather than being part of a seamless team of cooks hidden behind closed doors. The circular shape in this kitchen meant that food could be prepared facing into the room with constant eye contact with the whole family.

The tall ceiling partly came about because of the architect's vision for the outside appearance of the property. The architecture of the whole wing needed to be substantial in size. The cavernous interior, feeling a bit like a small church, was an initial concern. However, the clients feel very at home living in it. They luxuriate in the generous amount of interior space. Its expansiveness promotes well-being, and they can entertain without moving into other rooms. There are few problems with cooking smells which dissipate easily, and on hot or humid days – of which there are plenty in Memphis – the tall ceiling helps keep the space cool.

The cooking and preparation have a good work flow, and the distances between key activities and storage (there is a pantry behind the long wall) are under control. There has been no attempt to make this into an elaborate, professional or restaurant-style cooking kitchen with a gadget-a-minute on display. An appliance garage was installed within the culinary area, against the central back wall, to back up the main circular counter, and this removes the sometimes unsightly small appliances from view as well as providing valuable extra work surface, which can be hidden with a pull of the tambour.

The space feels like a combination of a living room, library and café that one might find in a relaxed country hotel.

OPPOSITE & ABOVE The clients wanted a practical working kitchen but within a large sociable space. A formal fireplace acts as the counterpoint opposite the culinary circle – a traditional focus for a relaxing area.

RIGHT The amount of floor area used for non-cooking activities was well over 50 percent.

PREVIOUS PAGES The curved counter makes a clear distinction between the cooking and relaxing areas and is aided by the hanging rack – necessary in such a large space as this. It also provides excellent lighting definition at night.

soft geometry
and its new partners
a strategy for designing humane kitchens in tight spaces

Soft geometry is the use of curved shapes that enable the whole space to work more efficiently and makes for easy movement around the kitchen environment. Although soft geometry is covered in the section entitled Kitchen Works: Design Analysis, it is worth discussing here in the context of a real project and in conjunction with other philosophical design tools. A recent new sister concept of soft geometry is ergonomics – body-centered design that uses the measurements of the human body to support the functions of everyday life. Vitruvius and the classical traditions of architecture used the golden mean to form the principle of proportion and scale, which was centered around the human figure. Today, we use it in a more practical way.

In considering human ergonomics – the planning of the space according to humane values – we have been exploring ways of encouraging communication and greater enjoyment of kitchen space. This involves setting up good sightlines between the table and cooking place; the identification of a priority position from which you can see visitors on arrival as well as having a long view across a landscape, garden or urban space. It also includes places to perch or linger, easy movement, choosing materials that reflect light well, and colors that cheer you, and conveying a feeling of quality in the construction of the furniture. In summary, it is all that encourages ease of use, comfort and flow.

this added to the exciting challenge of working on a contemporary design within it.

The plan opposite shows how a little bit of the hallway was used to increase the main culinary area, enabling us to use a soft geometry–based design. The space was restricted and is about as small as we can go to make this circular cabinetry work (there is a diameter of approximately 1 foot across the main curved counter). The oval center island is as small as it can be before it becomes useless, but it works for the couple who live here, certainly until (and if) they are blessed by hordes of children arriving!

There is easy movement through the circular corridor between the perimeter counter and its centerpiece, promoting a sense of enjoying passageways because you are safely guided. No sharp edges are there to cause any demands for peripheral vision, which is the way so much kitchen design fails – especially at pinch points or in narrow spaces. The worst place for sharp corners is on centrally located pieces of furniture or peninsulas. By their position they are always obstacles, and sharp corners alert peripheral attention. Curved, smooth edges, on the other hand, are so much better because the body relaxes instead of being threatened.

A lot of movement inside rooms is linked to avoiding objects or furniture, but when you have a chance to start from scratch and redesign your kitchen or any other room falling over furniture seems a poor end result. The principal way of maximizing movement and traffic flow is to limit the amount of furniture, to keep the space between pieces wider enough to accommodate three bodies, and assume at least one will be moving. In approximate terms this is around 4 feet. Where space is at a premium reduce this to 3 feet which is just enough for two people moving around with one working at a counter.

Plan key kitchen tasks to allow the body to move with a sense of economy. Less is more in terms of kitchen use. Provision of miles of countertop space translates into a big working triangle. Minimal distances are more efficient; economy of distance means balance and easy transfer to and from different tasks. The arms stretch to only 6 inches, so any tasks that can be done within this sphere means maximum efficiency, and only your fingers do the walking.

In this kitchen there are two or three steps between the main activities. Small is beautiful. Outside on the fringes there is more surplus space, but making the main exit and

ABOVE The curved corridor between the perimeter sink cabinet and the oval island provides the security of route management as you are safely guided without sharp edges appearing or any activation of peripheral vision. Deflection rather than blockage, smooth edges rather than sharp corners, are so much better because the body relaxes and is not constrained or threatened.

In this Georgian house off the River Thames in Barnes, London, we needed to merge three small rooms into one to get a humane and practical kitchen space. A cluster of small rooms is impractical for easy living, as both cooking and sociability prove difficult. The claustrophobia of small spaces is evident when carrying out active tasks that involve a number of people. Achieving an easy flow around small spaces is one of the luxuries that our design studio can indulge in more easily than some others because we do not use furniture of any fixed size, shape or style. For this project, the merging of three spaces in a historically protected building such as this comes with restrictions, but

Curved sink cabinet completes the flow of the space as a practical continuous work surface. A false wall behind contains some useful hidden engineering to hold up the ancient structure of this historic building.

The oval island is the main preparation point in this challenging kitchen space, which looks smaller than it appears. A small, low-level shelf helps keep the work surface free and can be used for receptacles while prepping or for serving.

A shallow cupboard sits in front of a structural column and provides useful storage for herbs and cooking condiments. Shallow depth storage (here 4 inches) is underrated.

An appliance garage is positioned here in a disused corridor, thereby utilizing the awkward space by tapering its shape to allow for access to other storage. Fold-back doors allow it to be used as a work area if required.

Borrowing floor space from the hall. A three-quarter height wall screen shields the cooking zone from view of the front door, bringing vital additional floor space into the culinary zone.

The drum wraps itself around the corner between two of the original rooms and provides capacious storage and a pleasant transition between the kitchen and eating area.

The table has good sightlines to the culinary area and is well supported by an extra drinks fridge, and storage hutch for table-related china. Although relatively snug, it still feels comfortable, lighter and is a destination rather than a hallway.

soft geometry and its new partners **49**

A cluster of small rooms is totally impractical for today's easy living – cooking and sociability would be difficult.

entrance outside the culinary circle helps eliminate any through traffic.

We tried to complement the soft geometry in the choice of materials; using a pale wood such as sycamore made the perimeter of the curved sink run reflective light, relaxing on the eye, while the centerpiece of dark rich ebony created a visual contrast. To be playful and gain more work surface, we made it oval in shape and tilted the wider side away from the sink area and main perimeter cabinet.

A contemporary aesthetic for the kitchen was requested but without compromising on color, soft shapes and high-quality craftsmanship. The clients were eager to enjoy cooking when they had the time to do it and to engage with friends as they toiled! The space is economical around the inner "ring road" (cooktop and sink area), but lingering opportunities exist around the drum cupboard and there is an uninterrupted sightline to the table.

Looking back on the project now, I can't imagine how we would have combined the spaces together so easily, created a clear destination for the culinary area, and avoiding eating up too much of the already modest hallway without the principles of soft geometry. I feel grateful to the clients for believing in the idea. The merit in any design is through its use and the qualities it brings for a more human-friendly environment. I hope that it speaks for itself in these pages.

OPPOSITE & ABOVE Generous slate and space between the insets make for relaxed cooking. A stainless steel upstand bends easily to the curved plaster wall to protect from grease splashes. Three small alcoves face the cook, but only one is a real window so the cook has a peephole through which to view the hall. A polished plaster finish adds a tactile luster to its curved shape.

LEFT Soft geometry is enhanced by appropriate woods and finishes. The island, for example, is made from dark woods – a walnut work surface on the low level shelf and ebony on the curved drum sides.

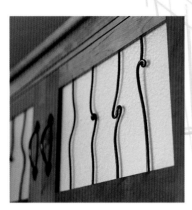

graceful locations
a new chamber in an old vessel

OPPOSITE Buried in the bowels of a late 17th century house, this kitchen has been carved out of three unused cavelike pantries. The upper house remains intact, with its elegant rooms of paneling and tall windows. Each piece of kitchen furniture was created with consideration for its weight and texture as well as its function and shape. They form collegiate groupings.

Like most individuals who notice their surroundings, I approach old buildings with a graceful respect. They have acquired veneration with age. Working in a William and Mary house dated around 1690 was a particular treat. The proportions of the rooms on three and half stories of hand-cut stone blocks are tall and square, well lit and ordered with elegant moldings and fireplaces. The rooms have a modest demeanor. They aren't large – just adequate by today's standards of spacious living, but they are not small either. There is a clear sense of order that you dare not disturb.

In order to make a decent size kitchen we confined ourselves to the more or less abandoned, musty basement, formerly three pantries that would have originally served as the domestic hub of the house. Hollowing out this series of ramshackle, cavelike enclosures – they could barely be described as rooms – we decided to carve out a single space running right across the house. As a blank canvas, the space remained in a semi-basement, which gave us cause for concern due to the lack of natural light.

The clients had a great love for old buildings. Andre Vrona is a master stonemason who runs one of Britain's most accomplished stone construction companies and regularly takes his team to Oxford and Bath for his work in England, as well as the U.S. for special projects to build houses in stone. With a great interest in the innate quality of materials

Cooking recess. This proved a natural location for the Aga range as there was one there previously. A small window gives much needed light, the stone quoins and timber beam frame it in a picturesque but delightful and traditional way.

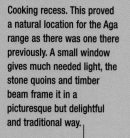

Tea and coffee console table with its cabinet above houses a small sink – that is hollowed out of a single piece of Ancaster stone. The legs and supporting structure are made of cast iron and finished with boot wax.

The island has three zones: a) The preparation area made of end grain maple and stainless steel is screened by a piece of solid Carrara marble that delineates the island into three sequences.

b) A low level table area for setting down shopping bags and food in transit.

c) A marble-covered storage cabinet used for additional preparation and for serving. Beneath the marble surface, deep drawers house all manner of utensils, flatware and cookware.

Asymmetrical walk-in pantry provides useful storage for dry goods. It is constructed from solid walnut with burl walnut panels, except on top where vertical metal spokes let in air and light.

A solid stone sink of Ancaster stone with oiled oak cabinet below. The finishes complement each other and will wear together gracefully, eventually looking as if they were made the same time as the original building.

Mondrian-inspired dishwasher and china storage cabinet. The 1950s pale color palette reflects more light into the room and gives an edge to the more traditional aesthetic of the other furniture pieces.

The "Court Cupboard" is made from cherry and hides two built-in refrigerators. Side cupboards add to the mass of the construction as well as providing useful storage. The bent metalwork suggests some age, and the acid-washed glass brings some brightness back into the room.

(being a stone carver himself) and with his wife Caroline's aesthetic sensibility for old and new alike, we had an immediate commonality with which to create a design for this ancient structure.

The house was built by a captain of the Lutine. Sadly, his ship was sunk before he moved in. The good captain went down with it and it resulted in the first claim made against the fledgling Lloyd's Insurance syndicate. The ship's bell was rescued and today resides in the famous Lloyd's building in London (designed by Richard Rogers) and is rung when any ship around the world sinks. Captain Skyner did not live to enjoy his house, but for many generations others did and still do. It sits high in its Lincolnshire village with expansive views across the landscape.

There was plenty of inspiration to be had from this graceful old building. The effects of weather and time were evident on both the outside and within, although the fabric of the house remains relatively complete. The copious paneling is worn, patched, distorted and elegant. The floors

are cracked and split, with visible patina of its years of enduring foot use. The textures of the plasterwork with uneven surfaces combine to make it a house of settled textures and friendly surfaces. All of these gave us a good foundation for our design language for the kitchen. The key design concept was an extreme version of the unfitted kitchen, wherein each piece of furniture would have consideration for its weight and texture as well as its function and shape. They were to form collegiate groupings, each with its own character.

The length of the room, the one modest window and the position of the flue gave us clear starting points to generate a plan. The sink was positioned in the recess in front of the window. A grid cupboard which was to house the dishwasher was partly excavated out of the thick wall, and we conserved enough wall space to place a large cupboard adjacent without blocking out too much light. We were keen to amplify the light into the room, so by using pale, pastel colors we not only created a collage of complementary hues

ABOVE LEFT
A tenuous synergy between the different aesthetics of the individual elements only becomes apparent to those with a poetic approach to design.

ABOVE RIGHT
Opposing and unexpected combinations of materials meet. Stainless steel, Carrara marble, cherry wood, Mondrian colors, Ancaster stone, old stone quoins, oak cabinetry – this is a personal and careful reflection of mixing old with new after many conversations with the clients.

Bigger rooms can accommodate more activities within sight of each other. This means better communication and an opportunity for a more accomplished kitchen design.

across the cupboard doors that reflected light from the window, but also minimized the scale of the piece. The soft 1950s colors of the Mondrianlike cupboard also complemented the natural tones of the solid stone sink.

A curved and solid low Carrara marble wall in the middle of the island creates of a touch of luxury and pleasure. Its rationale is explained somewhat as providing the configuration of the different working surfaces. Weighing two tons and magnificent as a standalone natural object, it was possible to install only in a basement. The sheer weight of it anchored the island that linked it to its colleagues, the solid stone slabs from which were carved the basins and surfaces that formed the two sinks nearby. Made from oiled oak, the sink cabinet matched the Ancaster stone – pale brown, with flecks of white and dark brown – textured and rough.

A new floor was laid in the same stone as the sinks – all of which came from a small local quarry that Andre had helped revive. Ancaster is from a low porosity limestone seam. The quarry opens for a short time in the summer when conditions are right. This keeps it small in scale and is environmentally less invasive.

A mature walnut tree in the grounds of the house had to be felled because it was unsafe, and was then dried and cut for use in the kitchen furniture. Other wood was selected for its individual qualities. All the furniture was custommade by an individual craftsman who followed it right the way through. Although modern machining techniques were used for preparation, a lot of the work involved was carried out by hand and required skillful and painstaking assembly. This is visible in the hutch and walk-in pantry where the curved shapes required special jigs.

The dark patina of the metalwork in the upper panels of the "Court Cupboard" (created by dipping the bars in wax while still hot from forging) give the sense of being in a medieval basement. Indeed, the heavy ceiling beams and the outcrops of exposed rough hewn stone around the chimney-like cooking area and at various points around the walls help to preserve the atmosphere of being in a very old, and partly sunken building.

This sociable kitchen concealed within the depths of the home has given part of the house a new focus, making it suitable for modern living. The upper house remains intact, untouched. The fabric has been carefully restored throughout by Andre and Caroline.

Respect for age does not mean avoiding the use of modern ideas or introducing new fabrics. Applying the same criteria that the original makers started off with, a belief in their own techniques, design ideas, and using the newest skills available is what is appropriate. Optimism about our own values, without change for its own sake, trying out new ideas and applying contemporary sensibilities is the best form of respect we can pay to old buildings.

OPPOSITE Inspired by a medieval cupboard, this dark walnut corner pantry with its metal dowels sits in its dark corner as if it were always there.

LEFT The weight of this dazzling piece of Carrara marble could only be appropriate in a basement kitchen. It sensuality belies its feeling of permanence and makes the cabinetry around it feel delicate.

PREVIOUS PAGES To increase the opportunity for natural light to occupy as much of the room as possible, a limestone floor was laid and pastel paintwork and pale woods chosen for the cabinetry.

eccentric spaces
unusual spaces inspire great ideas

The cultural pedigree of this extraordinary home is so unusual and varied, it defies description. Eccentric is an inadequate description, too, and I use it only because of the way it defies normal boundaries, and the labels we use to describe buildings, homes and their style. Is it a barn, a giant log cabin, an open plan loft, a series of tree houses or a timber-framed farmhouse? In terms of basic fabric, it is a series of wooden Japanese farmhouses on giant stilts. Made in California and transported to England in kit form, these houses have been erected in an abandoned quarry in Cambridge as a private home, where the structures are linked by a bridge, and surrounded by water, wild meadows and self-seeded trees.

I was invited to work on this kitchen, which turned out to be one of the most exciting design challenges I've experienced. Few houses (the word seems inappropriate, since it is more like a settlement where the landscape forms a major impact wherever you are – inside or outside) have aroused for me such feelings of uniqueness, lack of

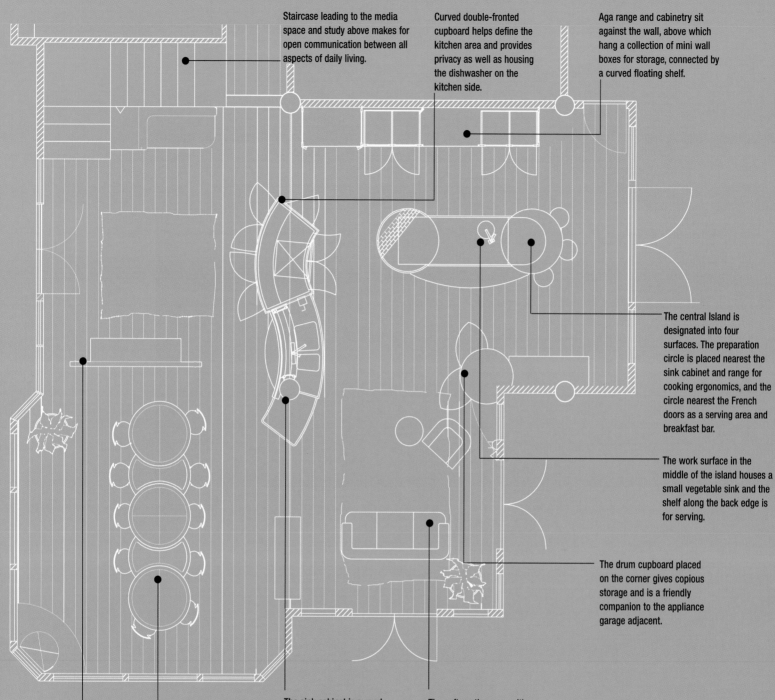

Staircase leading to the media space and study above makes for open communication between all aspects of daily living.

Curved double-fronted cupboard helps define the kitchen area and provides privacy as well as housing the dishwasher on the kitchen side.

Aga range and cabinetry sit against the wall, above which hang a collection of mini wall boxes for storage, connected by a curved floating shelf.

The central Island is designated into four surfaces. The preparation circle is placed nearest the sink cabinet and range for cooking ergonomics, and the circle nearest the French doors as a serving area and breakfast bar.

The work surface in the middle of the island houses a small vegetable sink and the shelf along the back edge is for serving.

The drum cupboard placed on the corner gives copious storage and is a friendly companion to the appliance garage adjacent.

A translucent glass screen suspended from the ceiling demarks an area as the entrance hall. The central window is mirrored glass and reflects light back into the dining area at night.

The "links" table made up of three identical circular tables with two butterfly intermediary tables. They can all be used separately or together in order to accommodate the right size appropriate to the number invited for dinner.

The sink cabinet is curved in the reverse way to its neighbor to bring movement into this dividing centerpiece. A touch of glamor is provided by cabriole legs on the end table.

The soft seating area with a chaise longue and sofa is a great place to relax especially in summer when both sets of French doors are open and the evening light comes pouring in.

PREVIOUS PAGES
Beyond the sink cabinet is a cozy sitting space. The normal rules of furnishing did not apply in this wooden Japanese-style longhouse as the large space offers huge freedom to choose different activity areas, but there is also a need to establish a clear, organized idea.

BELOW & RIGHT
Strong individual pieces of furniture, which took into account the eccentric qualities of the interior architecture as well as the scale and functional requirements, were an engaging challenge in this space.

grandness and peculiar originality. The interior spaces comprise part open plan, part barn dimensions, and are full of eccentric details borrowed from a log cabin. This is exciting for the first-time viewer, but for the clients the real challenge was how to organize their living habits to the best advantage and make themselves comfortable. The kitchen was the clear starting point.

The biggest of the buildings was chosen for the main living quarters. Guests and extra activities are in the other two. The amount of space available for the kitchen was generous, but much of the floor area was residual, with plenty of potential alcoves and no clear center. Exacerbated by no fireplaces, it was a difficult building to make yourself feel comfortable in. The need for familiar zones, fire circles or designated areas for different activity was apparent. The eccentricity of the interior begins with its continuous windows, including corners. They produce multiple sightlines as well as limit the space for placing furniture. It also means an overexposure to the garden as one can be

seen from all sides of the property and from the back gardens of neighbors. The upstairs gallery with its alcoves built into the roof made the large volume of space more intimate and provided potentially useful upstairs spaces. The roof has a powerful presence throughout which, linked to the ever-present wooden surfaces, extols a sense of being in a log cabin or a boat, especially as the mighty columns penetrate through the center of the space like a mast to carry the weight of the roof. The sensation of being suspended above the ground on stilts, surrounded by decks and walkways is equally powerful. We were faced with a complex set of opportunities and awkward issues which, if not thought out

carefully, were potentially courting disaster. It is safe to say the normal rules of furnishing could not apply. When you are not clear what to do and where to do it, you can hardly expect an efficient use of space. This gives you huge freedom but a real need to establish a clear, organizing idea. Comfort is connected with order, even if it is hidden or submerged.

The area devoted to the culinary activity was the first location to be chosen – the south-facing French doors attracted the best aspect and as it was partially below the upper gallery, it felt secure. However, more visual privacy was needed, especially as the main entrance, and first

LEFT Design features here include faceted acid-etched glass with mirror backed swirls on the painted dishwasher cabinet; an Italian limestone on the sink top; stainless steel hanging gantry for lighting and small utensils; sycamore veneers on the sink cabinet façade, and soft geometry shapes combined with dedicated work areas to provide a sense of order on the island.

PREVIOUS PAGE LEFT View into main culinary area showing fridge and main preparation area. There was a desire to keep the circulation spacious, but not to have the distance too long to maximize easy cooking activity.

PREVIOUS PAGE RIGHT Although the wooden walls, floors and ceilings were beautiful and plentiful, and we built much of the furniture from wood like cherry and walnut, we also made efforts to provide contrast from its soporific effects by decorating some pieces with this painted pattern. It proved an eye-catching device to link the individual furniture pieces.

point of contact was right in front of the space. Once decided, this made us realize we had in effect created an entrance area or threshold for visitors to wait for invitation and further access into the building. A sense of order was emerging! To reinforce this we proposed a suspended and semitransparent screen to complete this area as a hall. This also helped with delineating the dining space behind it from the arrivals point. The last unused area was the far corner under the gallery, with double doors leading out in two directionsonto the deck. This would be an excellent place for a sociable seating area as it contained the possibilities of eye contact with anyone using the central island.

At times it felt as if we were designing virtual walls to delineate the activities. In an open plan space this is how one achieves order. One wall was semitransparent and suspended, the other, defining the cooking area, took the form of a double-fronted curved cupboard with reflective glass panels that stood below the upper level loft. Extending beyond this to form an "S" shape was the sink cabinet. A curved glass acid-washed screen provided additional privacy between the kitchen service area and the dining space. A plate rack is housed within the screen, through which the draining crockery cast agreeable shadows, especially at night. Linked into one of the giant columns, this hybrid piece of furniture now became connected to the fabric of the building.

The cooking area is dominated by the Aga, its neighboring cabinetry and its sequence of square "flying" cupboards, suspended from a wavy shelf. Too much wood can be become soporific so we took the opportunity of putting in a reflective glass tiled wall as a backdrop. The client is a gifted cook and a believer in simple, honest cooking methods. No extra cooktops or ovens were required. This helped keep down the amount of wall-based cabinetry and allowed us to install an appliance garage on the far side of the island. We completed this storage wall with a built-in bookcase and a drum cupboard on the corner. This provided much-needed storage for dry goods and eased the transition between kitchen and the sociable sitting area.

The island gave us the opportunity to design for a variety of functional needs focused around two circular surfaces: one a preparation area with an end grain block running through it, the other a breakfast bar. A footrest runs around the bottom to accommodate weary feet. The light from the French doors washes the surface of the island, and the bar makes a good place to sit away from the traffic of culinary activity at the other end. The low level area is used for serving, and the vegetable sink and mid-area work surface support the Aga cooking activity.

Above the kitchen is a generous gallery reached by stairs adjacent to the main entrance doors. Visible through the open balusters when seated at the snakelike, mobile set of mini-dining tables is a media den and a home office. When the children are at home in the evening or when it is a day for working at home, all the main activities can be done without leaving the main living space. The master bedroom is also reached off this gallery, making the upstairs a more private family area – all squeezed out of the roof space. There is the equivalent of a self-contained house lurking within the confines of this Japanese-inspired barn. The presence and possibility of so many activities makes the building full of life.

The wooden fabric of the inside and outside of the building lends a unique quality that is summed up best as comfortable and friendly, bringing a sense of composure and easy belonging. When designing the furniture, we talked about the amount of wood to be used and agreed that it would suit the ambience and fit in well as our choice of material. The tongue-and-groove paneling was American red cedar with American white oak floor boarding. We used American cherry, maple and walnut for the main pieces of furniture. They form a natural complement to each other in terms of color and density of grain pattern. We also used a small amount of English sycamore on the cabinetry as a complementary element, and an Italian limestone on the countertops; stainless steel was installed where appropriate and the large cupboard was given a painted finish to deflect from the light-absorbing qualities of the wood. We provided a number of display points for the clients to personalize the design with places for vases, sculptures and objets d'art, making the furniture friendly and less architectural. In addition, colored patterns added to the island and drum cupboard loosen up the seriousness of the furniture. The interior décor chosen by the client added the final excellent touch to make it into an original but welcoming environment.

The wooden fabric of the inside and outside of the building lends a unique quality that is comfortable and friendly, bringing a sense of composure and easy belonging.

a modern freestanding kitchen
a new kitchen planned within an old idea

The use of free-standing furniture is hardly revolutionary, but in kitchen design it was and probably still is. In terms of designing separate pieces for the kitchen, do we really want to go back from whence we came? "Is this really progress when fitted (continuous counter) kitchens are popular and represent modern design and production techniques so well?" Susan Sera, an independent journalist, asked me recently in an interview. She went on to write a most articulate piece about the phenomenon of "unfitted" for her kitchen industry magazine.

I explained that it's not going back; it's going forward and improving upon a traditional, uncomplicated and natural way of designing a room. Our forebears had a straightforward way of planning a room. It was called furnishing – each piece was chosen for its function or its availability. The difference with the unfitted kitchen is that pieces are ergonomically designed to accommodate specific tasks, whether for cooking, cleaning up, storage, display or a range of social functions. So the kitchen appears as a collection of furniture pieces that, on close inspection, have a sound functional relationship. We describe this ergonomic concept as a dedicated work area.

Most kitchens are poorly planned. Inadequate design thinking goes into making what is a very demanding, highly used space work properly. Even in well-planned fitted or continuous counter kitchens, there is a new demand for the space being a living room and not just as a culinary workspace. When I launched the "Unfitted Kitchen" in 1986 through a company called Smallbone, it was an immediate hit with the public because it recognized that the kitchen was a room to live in, and a lot of decisions need to be made with that in mind. It has as its core value the spirit of home. Good ergonomics do not have to be sacrificed either, as

An orderly arrangement of a sink cabinet with stainless steel continuous surface, raised height dishwasher cabinet to the left with storage for china above and adjacent plate rack.

The free-standing range has a stainless steel pan storage rack on each side. The slate mantle behind frames a light colored mosaic center that reflects light back onto the cooking surface. Ranges need to have an architectural device to differentiate them from cabinetry – or they lose their position of authority in the heirarchy of traditional kitchen planning.

A central island in one of my favorite configurations – three levels for chopping, general preparation and a backup cooktop and low-level area that can be used for multiple tasks.

The Sub-Zero fridge is positioned to counterbalance the cabinetry on the back wall on the far side of the sink unit.

This window cupboard and seat was designed to emphasize it as a piece of architecture as well as offering a resting place to chat or read, taking advantage of the natural light from the window.

Curved walk-in pantry that provides substantial storage and takes the pressure off the rest of the room for extra cabinetry in maple and mazur birch with walnut details.

Dining and social room has a partly glazed ceiling to create extra light. The step down between the spaces determines a change of mood and function.

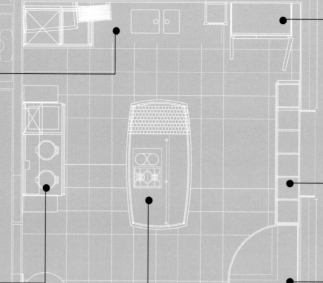

you can identify basic requirements for work surfaces, storage and controlling distances between key activities using simple techniques of analysis.

The orthodoxies in the kitchen industry have sprung from the convenience of manufacturers and retailers. The whole ideological basis of good design is that it works well for people, the users. Designers are trained to work toward the idea that design makes our lives work better through convenience and pleasure. So why hasn't the unfitted kitchen taken over? It has had a great impact on the market and loosened up kitchen design, paving the way for the next big move – toward becoming a living room. It gives so much more flexibility and opportunity for varied, original and efficient design. The recent use of casters to make furniture pieces portable is one way to create the illusion of unfitted – another is the nonmatching mix of colors, woods, and materials offered by many kitchen companies, that enable furniture pieces to stand out in their own right, rather than blending seamlessly and rigidly into the constraints of traditional kitchen cabinetry.

So what are the drawbacks? The main issue for designers and clients is that the unfitted kitchen requires a lot more thought than rows of counters. The kitchen industry doesn't like it because their modular units don't have end panels. They are keen on façade-driven counters placed mostly around wall perimeters. Free-standing furniture is harder to make because it has to be constructed for viewing from three sides; it needs to co-relate; and standardization of sizes is much harder.

ABOVE The dishwasher cabinet on the left is expressed as a separate piece of furniture with its hand-painted plaid front. The solid wood columns of the ripple sycamore sink cabinet give weight to the façade.

RIGHT A small metalwork panel offers charm and individuality to the door panels on the window cupboard.

FAR RIGHT Modern houses suffer from a loss of deep walls that you find in older buildings. This window furniture redresses that; it naturally frames the view and creates a perching point at the heart of the room.

Designers are also afraid or do not understand how to deal with the air space surrounding the pieces, particularly in corners. They need to think about creating individual pieces, each with its own characteristics. This assists with another important but often ignored sensibility: The architecture needs respect. The corners of a room define the space, and trying to leave at least two freely visible seems kind to the building. A feng shui expert I met in a showhouse in New York told me that this is very compatible with the concept of energy or people getting trapped in corners – so it is important to leave them open. In Western terms we would say that our furniture traditions also require space and that corners were places that were on the edge of the room – away from the center and therefore an unaccommodating place to be doing things. It is important, therefore, to appreciate the opportunities and subtleties of buildings in order to help identify if an unfitted kitchen is in keeping with the fabric of the house.

In the past, furniture was a luxury of the rich; poor people had to make do with a few pieces. If you were lucky enough to own any noteworthy item, you would put it on display, like spoon racks in the 17th century. Domestic furnishing invoked the collecting of furniture as and when you could afford it. The pleasure of that has now largely been taken away, although we as a design studio often carry out master plans for clients, enabling them to purchase pieces over time. The unfitted approach is also great for people who want to use old pieces, antiques, or incorporate something different, although it is often hard to find individual pieces with the right dimensions that satisfy demanding functional requirements.

Variety is the key to the concept. Mixing woods, styles, materials, heights, shapes and color are the currency. Sameness, repetition, modularity are the drivers of the design, and rigid geometry are its enemies! Kitchens are places for people to live, not just for them to cook as some kind of automaton. Kitchens are an expression of individuality and comfort.

The unfitted concept is a democratic, civilized and easy-to-live-with concept. I believe it has a great future because it has morphed into the sociable kitchen. And as the kitchen has now taken over as the new living room, absorbing all the downstairs functions of the home, I feel the foundations have been laid for a future design concept for the home that is humane and flexible.

During the planning of this new house for Keiran and Pamela, we looked at using a relaxed modern aesthetic to emphasize the spacious qualities of the tall ceiling that is open to the roof, which in turn would make up for the less spacious floor area. The main culinary area was a little tight for a generous approach to sociable kitchen design. The frees-tanding furniture idea was not pushed hard. Having planned for a central island so that you could look at the dining table and out to the garden, we needed to create substantial storage space, especially as a fair

As a planning idea, the unfitted kitchen is flexible, respectful of the architecture, friendly, and creates a sound ergonomic basis for creating groups of related activities.

amount of wall space was sacrificed to windows and door openings. A walk-in curved corner pantry allowed us to make a special feature out of the window – a seat surrounded by useful storage compartments made a welcome and central place to sit for chatting or relaxing while someone is cooking.

The fridge, free-standing and standing in its constructive shell of light-reflecting stainless steel, does not look too dominant, just natural placed for easy access. The Aga, too is surrounded by simple shapes and material choices. Gently curved sideboards on each side of the Aga augment its surface area for storing cooking utensils. A simple green slate surround filled in with mosaics and topped with a curved cover piece brings continuity and freshness to this back wall, where the junction between the flue and ceiling was potentially awkward.

Unfitted kitchens can be as modern or traditional as the owners wish in aesthetic terms, but as a planning idea, I believe that it is up-to-the-minute. It is flexible, respectful of the architecture, friendly and creates a sound ergonomic basis for creating groups of related activities. It allows for designing some specially tailored pieces to a precise specification, in this case, the island and the window cabinet. By using a combination of old pieces of furniture, or simply just creating a room in a traditional way of assembling functional pieces in the best format for living, you can do it yourself. And you can take the furniture with you when you move – if you wish. I hope you agree that this is a concept with a sound future.

LEFT Simple clean lines with a touch of soft geometry make for easy circulation. These large but different pieces of furniture show that being unfitted doesn't always have to mean that they need space around them to create the experience of a furnished room.

a modern freestanding kitchen 73

better on a boat
potentials and pleasures of confined spaces

Why live on a boat when you can afford an elegant stucco townhouse in London's Notting Hill or a rooftop apartment overlooking the Bay Bridge in San Francisco? Living on a boat is the equivalent of a mobile home on the water. Its cramped conditions are moderated by the quiet buoyancy of being on water. Can this measure up to the comparative spatial freedom of an average house with a well-proportioned interior and a yard beyond in which to extend one's living space?

To enjoy living in small spaces, you need to revel in order, at the expense of free and easy living. You can't be profligate with space or accumulate things on a whim or doubtful need. You can't hoard or build on extensions. This need for order quickly becomes self-motivating. The need for economy in matters of storage and practical activity gives life on a boat different priorities. You focus on the outside environment to offset cabin fever and attempt to enjoy the restrictions by embracing the idea of compactness. Like living in a small apartment or a mobile home, small is not so much beautiful, but necessary.

One's closeness to the ever-present hull, the low ceilings and the feeling of being enclosed affects your eyes, your hands, and your feet – as well as your head! Everywhere the active parts of the body are close to the physical fabric of your environment and make an impact on your sense of movement. You need to take pleasure from this in order to make the whole business of living in this restricted space bearable. You move more deliberately, distances are shorter for those active moments of household chores; you don't rush, but instead negotiate the obstacles with care, using your hands more frequently.

OPPOSITE
Miniaturized central island. The same principles of sociability apply as in a normal kitchen, getting the cook to face into the cabin. The tighter planning makes distances shorter, and every available nook and cranny is utilized, from the curves of the bow to the floor, which holds water tanks. Fridges and appliances are tucked in below the windows where the boat expands to form its full berth.

RIGHT Closeness to the ever-present hull, the low ceilings and the feeling of being enclosed mean the active parts of the body are close to the physical fabric of your environment and make an impact on your sense of movement. Good design helps you take pleasure from this with its order and efficiency. It should make the whole business of living in a restricted space bearable, even pleasurable.

All the qualities that you would want from a large luxurious house can be replicated in miniature – a sort of grown-up working dollhouse.

On a boat you must take its condition more seriously or ultimately it sinks! Maintenance is second nature, so there is a persuasive and positive interest in taking care of your physical environment and the instruments needed for nautical survival. They need to work reliably, to be well made and to last. The steering wheel can't be plastic, the engine needs to be in tip-top condition, the fixtures need to be solid stainless steel, not coated steel that rusts. The wood needs to be well finished to ensure durability and no splinters. Everywhere performance has to be exacting. A well-engineered, cared-for and efficient environment is a satisfactory feeling.

LEFT On a boat there is always the presence of water and close proximity to weather conditions. All the design elements had to fit in with the exterior shape of the hull, which is more restricting than in a conventional house, but can still be made enchanting to look at with the right sequence of materials and finishes.

BELOW The kitchen viewed from the salon through the railings that divide the two. The rough handmade metalwork creates an unexpected contrast to the precision of the main cabinetry.

Pull-out work surface adjacent to engine room door for use while cooking only.

Curved-sided cupboard containing oven, warming drawer, pull-out full height racks and pantry storage above.

Sink area with view across the water; dishwasher recessed inside expanded hull. Specially shaped sinks maximize available space. Mosaic backsplash works well with the shape and scale of the boat.

This tapered cabinet is designed around the windows to incorporate a tall china cabinet, air conditioning units, a dishwasher and space for bottle storage.

Bottle storage, china and cooking equipment cupboard, and air conditioning ducts are housed in this area. Construction of the paneling is mostly in sycamore.

Exit stairs to main deck and poop deck.

Two fridges and deep freezer are recessed here into the hull along with a window seat for perching, and heat exchange units and their attendant cabling.

The central island houses a Viking six-burner range, a 4 foot circular drum for preparation with a Nero granite surface, and a capacious rack below for pan storage. Serious cooking can be done in this kitchen.

A pop-up projector is built into this coffee table, height cabinet and a screen that comes down from the opposite central cabin wall can be lowered electrically.

The salon is situated between the culinary zone, and the bedrooms can be reached through double doors shown at the bottom of the plan. The furniture becomes slightly grander with richer veneers such as burl elm and the space is furnished with comfortable leather chairs and a couch.

LEFT There is still room for a free-standing table and chairs, which provide more flexibility than a built-in option. The swirling pattern on the glazed cabinet was inspired by light reflection on water.

Space planning needs to be engineered carefully, as distances between things are minimized and not just where you can see, but also where you can't, for example, in lockers, between the curves of the hull or below deck where the water tanks are housed. Every square inch must be used, considered, filled, planned and ruminated over. Utilitarian requirements, services, and desire for living spaces all must work to maximum effect. Planning access for maintenance to functional gadgets on board means that panels have to slide and floors need hatches. Boat design commands an accomplished understanding of ergonomics and the science of measurement, as well as a working knowledge of anthropometrics – how to support the human body in action. Applying these two areas of skill to this interior living space brought unsurprising results: it worked well in daily use.

The idea of emphasizing the luxury in small things as well as the bigger things was given careful consideration – from services such as air conditioning, music systems and a home theater, to professional-style cooking appliances, a well-designed kitchen preparation area, high-quality handmade furniture and comfortable arm chairs. The overall result was to give the experience of being in a well-furnished environment with its sociable side catered to in the adjoining salon, where excellent lighting, balanced use of colors and a relaxed choice of natural materials were key to achieving the right ambience onboard.

We planned to incorporate all the facilities of a normal house in this kitchen, simply on a smaller scale. The style the clients requested was for a comfortable modern aesthetic, but using hints of traditional detailing appropriate for a boat built around 1910. Much of the original fabric was used throughout the boat, but in the kitchen and the salon area there was little left of any value since it had originally been the cargo hold, probably used for coal or coke. The original living quarters had been tiny in what is now the bath alcove.

We installed a small central island for preparing, cooking and standing around to talk. Small perching points were built between the hull cupboards and around the air conditioning and heat exchange grills. Features added for use while cruising on the open seas include hinged bottle rack stays, gallery rails, secret door and drawer pin locks, blinds that work on sloping walls and a pull-out work surface that disappears when access to the engine room is needed. Appliances such as deep freezers and fridges were

hidden in the sides of the hull. To keep as much sense of openness as possible, the division between the kitchen and salon was kept visually open by using a railing – a roughly finished affair to reduce its engineering quality and emphasize its handmade appearance. It feels as if it is a relic from the original hold! Carpets and free-standing furniture were employed where possible to imitate normal house furnishings.

So to make life better on a boat was our mission – with no disagreement from the clients. All the qualities that you would want from a large luxurious house were replicated in miniature – a sort of grown-up working dollhouse. That was the vision I had in my mind. We all have this instinctive appeal of childhood ready for recall. Small spaces or dens, camps and retreats have the same root. Home represents a sanctuary as well as a building working hard for our physical comfort.

The appeal of this Dutch barge was the microcosm of all these rolled together, plus one. It moves around, friction-free in uncongested water lanes, marine life beckoning, and ready for mooring at erstwhile ports, new landscapes presenting themselves as replicas of views painted by the likes of Turner or Canaletto for your living room walls.

ABOVE Stairs up to the poop deck are steep and narrow. Movement is carried out with consideration, although you get used to them and soon minimize these restrictions.

releasing design energy
brainstorming and creating anticipation

OPPOSITE View from the front porch shows the central island drum's dramatic placement as part of the long inviting view into the garden via the kitchen.

The first glimpse is exhilarating. Then comes one of quiet excitement when you walk through the door, your antennae picking up the expectation of what is to come and your eyes busy with the sparkle of anticipation. You have arrived at a beautiful place, a house, apartment or cottage with an atmosphere and nobility of its own. You can feel the care and energy that has been put in to bring such wholeness to the surroundings.

What are the qualities that make your body go into pleasure mode, lighten your feet so you move easily and make your hands reach out to feel your surroundings? Apart from desire, perhaps provoked by envy of size, prestige or sheer architectural splendor, what makes you feel well-housed and warm spirited? Big spaces, a rich mix of textures, antiques, beautiful paintings, light and well-proportioned rooms, unexpected touches and grand views – things that create memorable moments, picturesque vignettes.

On occasions when this happens, I am eager to capture and somehow reengineer what I have seen for later use. I keep these interior design memories in suspended animation for occasional recall. They become part of my mental library to be consulted during the creative process. Since I was a small child, I have been dressing and undressing buildings, furniture, domestic utensils of all kinds from pottery to glass, antique cooking equipment, and memorizing those that are different, unusual, out of the ordinary. We all have our own picture libraries and at times, such as when inventing new designs or redesigning your home space, they provide visual fuel for brainstorming – the method used by all creative people to foster new ideas. It may be a truism that there is rarely

Wet area piece. A unified sink cabinet, storage, and dishwasher designed for minimum walking. A raised-height dishwasher surrounded by generous cupboards for fast and easy unloading of china. The sink cabinet is constructed from sycamore with a plain black granite surface.

Giant scale grid cupboard. Designed to subsume the fridge, which is set into a wall cupboard with door panels, into the architecture of the tall space. The panels conceal everyday kitchen items, such as shelving for coookbooks, dry foods, a pull-out microwave and cooking equipment.

The original Georgian window has been made into a door to access the beautiful gardens outside.

Dishwasher drawers. These are incorporated into the mini kitchen to provide optional extra capacity when needed or for use when the main dishwasher is already in use.

Long central island in three sections. Dacor cooktop unit with downdraft rise and fall extractor is at the center flanked by copious work surfaces. A chopping block at the far end provides the opportunity to cook facing into the room. Low-level breakfast table in one piece of delicate Carrara marble.

Central drum. Visible from the front door to provide maximum visual effect, the drum helps pull your eye toward the view of the garden beyond. Rich ebony veneers and gold leaf banding with a walnut surface complement the Victorian detail of the kitchen interior.

Mini sink area. When the dining room is in full use, up to 30 people may need to be served. The tall drum cupboard houses china and glassware for the dining room which is itself low on storage space.

anything new and that all design is some kind of plagiarism. The best type of design work makes use of a multiple plagiarism where the design is not nailed down to one source, but instead has an element of connectedness and contains some unexpected counterpoints. There is a richness that is borne out of a liberating sense of place.

Located on the banks of the River Clyde near Glasgow, Scotland, this grand house is full of memorable vignettes. There are layers of history, and the last major makeover was in the late nineteenth century. A wealthy shipowner poured time and money in a typically Victorian manner into building a grand staircase, and adding rich moldings, gold burlap wallpaper, intricate paneling, ornate cast-iron radiators and monolithic marble fireplaces – with all of these features being inspired by a variety of historical periods, from Neoclassical to Regency Chinoiserie. It is a true example of the style known as Scottish Baronial.

We carved out a space from three old service rooms – the butler's pantry, the storeroom and a staff parlor – so that the new sociable kitchen could be at the center of the house and close to the dining room. This newly created room spanned a good part of the back side of the house and overlooks a substantial lawn. The bay window added in the Georgian period provided an excellent location for the dining table. The key to the design was a long central island with cooking facilities incorporated,

facing the lawn. Its position was decided by placing the circular drum cupboard directly in front of the main door from the hall, which in turn is the focal point from the door in the grand front entrance. Making clever alignments is one of the luxuries and necessities of big spaces and grand houses.

We don't need in-depth analysis of why everything looks the way it does in order to enjoy it. We have come through a period of design morality, and in these days of "anything goes," enjoying, watching (and conserving) history is the norm rather than trying to change it. Initially I found the interior a little overwhelming, but I soon realized that the current owners felt comfortable with the spirit of their Victorian heritage so I knew I had a good project on my hands. The originality and self-confidence of the architecture and interior vignettes gave a palpable energy to our senses and propelled us into a mood of confidence. New work should be exercised in the same spirit, a license

ABOVE Rich use of opposing materials makes for a dramatic and pleasing array of visual effects. The cast and slumped glass on the Sub-Zero fridge has been mirror backed and feels appropriate to the coldness associated with its function.

LEFT A view of the back-up washing up area. The dining room is to the right, and this area comes into use when the family are entertaining.

LEFT Generous parking
space is provided around the
cooking area, which faces
into the center of the room.
The drum in the center
houses glass and china for
the adjacent table.

OPPOSITE Rich ebony
veneers with a gold leaf
thumbnail molding case the
drum, itself made up of 10
microlayers of plywood and
veneer. These are evidence of
the craftwork that goes into
making the furniture, and link
with the Victorian sensibilities.

The originality and self-confidence of the architecture and interior vignettes gave a palpable energy to our senses and propelled us into a mood of confidence.

with history and a freedom to enjoy the unrestricted expression of a liberal design mentality. To let artists and designers get on with it and not do too much navel gazing is perhaps the most creative way to go and the best way of ensuring good work.

There are historical and period references in our furniture, but there is no explicit attempt at fostering it. We try to draw our design reference from its initial source. We acknowledged the surroundings by understanding the scale needed to make the furniture feel comfortable and the balance of materials, types of floor and the feelings of the family toward the space.

Barbara, the lady of the house, was full of enthusiasm for something different. She plunged into all sorts of fantasies and stuck to her Versace-inspired colors and patterns. As a serious and skilled cook, she wanted to be able to do corporate entertaining in the dining room, so we designed a secondary backup sink and storage area adjacent to the double swing dining room door. A sitting area around a wood-burning stove and the old family silver vaults left over from the previous room arrangement made a great atmosphere focus. The giant grid storage cupboard with molded mirror-glass bubbles on the fridge was lent a glamorous touch with its Versace pattern on the panels.

At the most crucial point in the design process, the whole design team had stood around the flat chest in our studio to brainstorm with three-dimensional drawings in front of us. Colors, textures, the ambience and random, new and unexpected ideas were brought into the design. How we do this is hard to explain, but a degree of humor, "anything goes" mental flexibility, a sort of freeform open-to-vulnerability idiocy finally gives the design some depth. The only rule is not to voice any criticism, except in a lighthearted manner. The process may not stand up to a lot of scrutiny, but it seems to work in harnessing the very elements that bring the kitchen space to life, thus releasing much-needed design energy. All projects benefit from this, as it gives spontaneity, originality, and uniqueness to the end result.

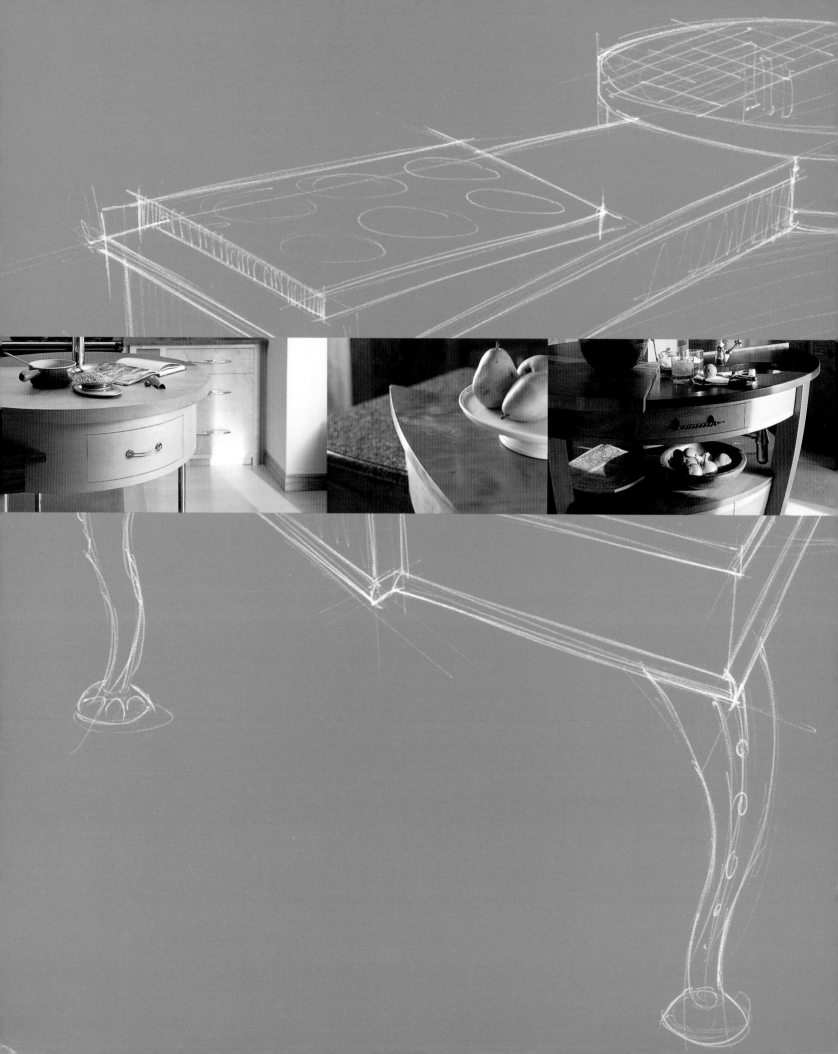

communication between space and people

When designing a table or chair, function is a given – essentially a platform of the right height and size. How you go beyond this is what gives it real life force. Likewise, kitchens that work are more than a platform to cook. That they need to function is also a given, but they must enhance life by becoming a place to automatically congregate – just being in them should raise one's spirits. Too many kitchens are dull and just filled with indifferent cabinetry, like commercial overspill. Enjoyment needs to seep out of the furniture. The rugged personal objects of home with their colors, shape, and textures should be crowding your peripheral vision. So, too, should aromas percolate from bowls of fruit on the dresser and simple evidence of kitchen life: in pots, pans, and postcards, which culminate to provide a visual montage into your private underworld retreat from everyday life, and keep the temperature of your home hospitality warm.

creating the right atmosphere
achieving style without prejudice

OPPOSITE Style discussions were kept decidedly open and low key. The client wanted a harmonious, forward-looking design, easy to live with, of modest manners but not derivative. That did not mean compromising the character of the layout or the style of the furniture pieces – on the contrary, it secured a sense of individuality, touches of quirkiness, and some original thinking.

I am asked on a regular basis if I design country kitchens or if my style is contemporary. As soon as people know you work in the domestic design sector, there are these questions that appear to spring to mind first, which often border on banality. I wonder whether it is possible to go beyond these labels or if they are of real value.

Clearly how things look is important, but it seems that what we see is the resonance of them, not the material thing itself. It's what we associate with a house, an item of furniture or a piece of fabric that gives us the picture in our heads. We feel or can touch the texture and the sculpture, but that is not what we really see. What is on our mind is its meaning to us, the big mental picture, and this is when the conversation about style begins. It helps us turn the story behind each object into identifiable labels.

I long for the day when the questions might be more on the lines of: "Are your kitchens easy to live in?" "Does the design improve house life?" "Why are your designs inspiring?" and "Will they make me feel uplifted?" "What kind of character can they have?" and "Does the design have multiple references. that is, does it have pedigree and subtlety, or is there visible depth or evidence of thinking depth?"

Often during a kitchen installation, before completion when we have installed the furniture, there is a moment when the pieces that are

Low-level table built below the narrow window to hold TV and focus the soft seating area.

Built-in cupboard to use space between structural columns and provide location for the home office area.

Home office area is planned carefully with storage computer links and a large work surface.

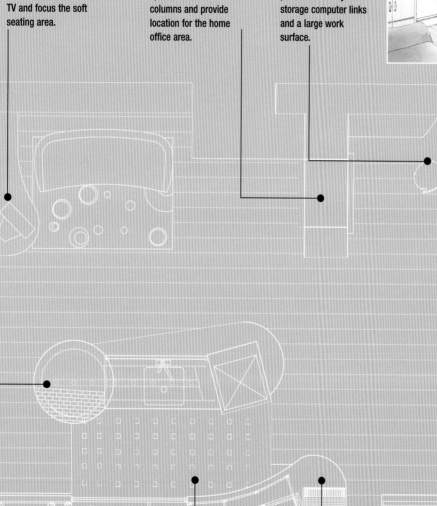

Central island integrated with sink cabinet. The glass back-splash conceals the domestic area from the entrance door, and the raised-height dishwasher is set at an angle on the right. Plenty of light bounces onto the island from the glass ceiling and the main French doors, making it a very pleasant place to stand.

The Aga is given a modern framework. Concrete pillars free-stand with a separate stainless steel hood and glass tiles behind.

A rubber floor finish was inserted in the main cooking and sink areas to provide more durability and comfort underfoot.

Appliance garage and china storage are housed within the curved cabinet with its circular table for setting down shopping bags. The plate rack sits in this unusual location and is used for displaying china.

The free-standing fridge in the dining area sits between the key working zone and the glass-fronted hutch in the dining area.

The table was positioned within the natural light from the French doors, and within eye contact of the island, soft seating area and home office.

unpainted look distinctly flat, some of the countertops are awaiting delivery, and the walls are only coated in a starter paint; the whole space looks lackluster and slightly disappointing. A few days later, with the paint finishes completed on the furniture and walls and with the countertops in place, the transformation is complete, everyone is happy. But I am irritated! This last microscopic change in surface treatment accounted for too much difference in effect. The earlier phase was when the real work was done. However, substance is not always rewarded. In design, it seems, surface counts for a great deal of the impact. Our eyes are more easily pleased from a distance than they are close up. So too are the associative aspects referred to above, or what you could describe as its anthropology. What is harder is to get a sense of the quality below the surface.

In this kitchen we designed for a family in Glasgow, Scotland, there was little design style discussion or what you could describe as prejudgment of style "anthropology." We kept the style discussions decidedly cool and loose. Caroline wanted a harmonious, forward-looking design, easy to live with and of quiet, modest manners. By this she did not mean dispensing with character, but instead to create a sense of individuality, touches of quirkiness and some original thinking, especially in the layout and furniture pieces. She was also very keen on the quality of craftsmanship, construction and choice of materials. The house is a Victorian merchant's villa with generous rooms but with an unappealing extension dating from the 1960s. This was the space designated for the new kitchen.

Caroline and I discussed the rebuilding of the extension, and, along with the help of an excellent local architect, we started to consider the layout of the kitchen. It is not radical in terms of kitchen design, but it provides for easy circulation. We made space for an island and calculated her kitchen needs. Caroline stuck to her guns about placing her cooking range, an Aga, against the wall. This meant the sink area would be in the island, something I tend to hold out against. It is good, though, to have one's prejudices challenged. By placing an opaque, sculpted glass screen we hid the sink from view from the entrance door. We placed a dishwasher immediately behind the right-hand end of the island, and in the wall behind, a china cabinet and plate rack. There was only one step between the sink and the dishwasher.

Individual touches included a series of abstract designs,

handpainted sink cabinet door panels, visible only once you come into the cooking zone. Metal shaped bars on several cabinet doors created a linking element, while some excellent concrete and stainless steel work allowed us to make the hanging racks and extractor canopy in the shape we wanted. Our furniture makers did a superb job of making complicated curved pieces, including the sloping tambour on the front of the appliance garage.

In English law "without prejudice" means that you can write someone a letter without it being able to be produced in court as evidence to be used against you. You are free to make an offer or accusation without consequence. In applying this as a metaphor for designing interiors, you could say that you want to suspend judgment until the case (or the design) is complete or can be looked at as a whole.

ABOVE The drum is the focus for preparation – conveniently close to the sink. Its shape makes movement and use easy and no façades mean you can converse across the space is a more carefree manner.

In design, it seems, surface counts for a great deal of the impact. What is harder is to get a sense of the quality below the surface.

The case to be judged is the house architecture, as the shell and provider of light; the interior architecture, for its planning and quality of movement in the space; the furniture for its size, use, and sculpture, and the interior decoration providing the tone, color, and ambience. All sorts of criteria will be applied: from whether it works on a logical level to whether it feels good to be in, from the quality of the craftsmanship, to its use when entertaining and how it will age. If it is successful, it has to have that "X" factor – does it all work together?

I often find that having my prejudice broken is thoroughly pleasurable because it means you have learned something. It is hard at first and while you make mental adjustments, but afterwards, it adds a whole new dimension to the way one thinks.

ABOVE Working sensitively around the architecture at the junction between two rooms, we had several small functions to solve – backup storage for china in the tall narrow cupboard, a small table for unloading shopping to the fridge and a plate rack for backup to the dishwasher.

RIGHT The use of different glass panels and handmade metalwork adds to the individuality of each piece of furniture.

FAR RIGHT Detail from the island. The screen provides extra privacy, and the different levels express order for use of the work surfaces.

RIGHT The curve on the appliance garage base in the foreground brings extra capacity, and eases you in smoothly to the main culinary zone. Light bounces down from the skylight, and the glazed triangle in the new pitched roof void gives the room a pleasant and spacious atmosphere.

a sense of place
how the outside affects the inside

How far do you take the locality into account? A kitchen is deep inside the home, an inward-looking enclosure at its heart. Its milieu is described best by adjectives such as nurturing, private, sustenance and sociable. Does the outside world matter very much when you are indoors?

Does the outside inform the inside? The scale of the building is a helpful starting point, but the best clues come from the description of the building's type – it nearly always includes its location in its name. If it is a cottage the countryside is implied; a townhouse is at the center of a town or city, a beach house is clearly near the sea – the external setting is evocative and meaningful. Siting houses is an art that seems to have fallen by the wayside. When houses were built in isolated positions before the days of subdivisions and crowded landscapes, its position was carefully considered to have shelter from prevailing winds, big views across landscape for defensive reasons and access to supply routes, water and towns. Today for those fortunate enough to find virgin land on which to build, the position of the site will be determined by local planners or by privacy. For the vast majority of home buyers, the starting point is choosing the location. It's the most decisive influence on how we would like to live, the setting or environs for our daily experience of moving in and around our home. A sense of belonging to a place is a deep psychological need; without it we are rootless. Choice of location is a part of our personal emotional territories, such as being near other members of the family, our favored landscape or park, our desire to be near water or in a beautiful street, to be part of a safe or activity-rich neighborhood, or simply pragmatic requirements like being near work or good schools. The choice of house

RIGHT We may not be able to choose a site for a new house, but we can choose where to live – the locality. A sense of belonging to a place is a deep psychological need; without it we are rootless. It is exhibited here by this farmhouse in Burgundy from where Aubert and Pamela De Villaine have developed a superb vineyard within the local environs.

has to fall within what is available within these boundaries.

When Aubert and Pamela asked us to design a kitchen located in a set of old farm buildings in an ancient Burgundian village in the heart of French winemaking country, the impact of the location was overwhelming. Its *raison d'être* is the valuable *terroir* within the vicinity. This means not just its physical position on a southfacing slope, but the special quality of the soil, particularly including its underlying 30 feet of substrata. The roots of the vine feed from deep down. The quality of the grapes is affected by feeding on its mineral content, so the place as well as its climate is important. Wine harvests are well known to be affected by sun, frost and bacterial conditions, but you can't affect the *terroir*. It is there, unchangeable with its immense history and economic value, understood and developed since the days of the Romans.

Aubert and Pamela managed their vineyard and ran their wine harvests from their home property. We had to design a living kitchen that was appropriate for a French wine grower's way of life. The fabric of the property comprised a collection of working stone buildings – erected through hard work and need – built around the contours of this hilly outcrop of the Burgundian countryside.

The space was not large, and we had much to incorporate. Careful dissemination of the wish list meant that we could fulfill the design only by making some reductions in the size of furniture pieces. The clients were great cooks and wanted a fireplace they could use for cooking. A local company had developed a raised-height open hearth that could double as a grill. We agreed to design a traditional stone fireplace around it, which, while taking up much valuable space, provided a great focal point.

With no room for an island, an oval-shaped peninsula was chosen, echoing the line of maximum floor space available that was compatible with movement around the center of the kitchen and still allowing space for a dining table.

The property was built over different periods, nestling into the sloping sides of the upper village road leading into the heart of the village. The front door was on the road and hardly ever used, leaving the kitchen entrance, reached up some stone steps from the main yard, to be the main thoroughfare into the house. So the kitchen was the welcoming point, the hallway-threshold into the family environment. To provide a welcoming pause and a storage place for boots, hats and coats, we created a stepped cupboard by the door. By making it double sided, we could create backup storage for china since the dishwasher was

LEFT The kitchen is also the entrance hall to the property. The stepped cupboards provide some privacy from the entrance door and offer purpose-driven storage on both sides.

A raised hearth sits in the newly constructed stone fireplace. This incorporates a cooking facility. The metalwork, made locally, provides control of the heat and position of logs to allow grilling or spit roasting. A fat drip tray is built into the front edge.

A circular peninsula for preparation and serving allows for the largest surface with the least disruption to movement. The room is not big enough for an island.

The sink in front of a window affords wonderful views across the valley. Different surfaces define the activities. Stainless steel covers the sink area.

Oven and raised height dishwasher and china storage fill this crowded cupboard, with a plate rack mounted on the side for extra storage capacity.

The structural column is what remains of the wall between the two rooms. We made use of it by placing a fridge inside the gap – giving the table a little extra privacy.

The stepped cupboard has china storage on the kitchen side, and one cupboard houses a mini TV. On the back near the entrance door, the lower three cupboards provide space for shoes and boots.

Entrance door into outside porch which has a café table and chairs for eating alfresco.

This court cupboard doubles as a pantry for dry goods and large cooking utensils. The extended base offers a temporary spot for shopping bags and removing outdoor footwear.

RIGHT Around the main cooking area we tried to leave the walls as free as possible to let the new fireplace and original architecture have presence. The tiles were reclaimed terracotta from a local source, and the few new beams we put into the ceiling were also reclaimed.

OPPOSITE The court cupboard frames the opening we made between the two original rooms and provides welcome additional storage.

BELOW The colorful stepped cupboard provides storage for a range of objects, from china to boots and even a small TV. Its surface is also for display of kitchen utensils. The sense of locality is enriched by the striking collection of Provençal-inspired patterns on each door panel.

immediately adjacent, a real example of where one-off custom-built furniture contributes so much to making a small space – with its demands for a high degree of function – work so much better than standard units.

French Provincial decorative traditions are distinct. They have long-standing languages based on craft techniques and vocabulary of detailing that are ring-fenced by time and historical association. A few key aesthetic decisions were made early. We were to use local woods. France is lucky to still have plenty of hardwood forest. Oak, ash and cherry trees are still available from well-forested areas of the countryside. The ambience of the kitchen was to feel French in the core materials chosen, from French ash cabinetry, olive wood panels, French granite work surfaces and reclaimed terracotta flagstones on the floor. The impact of the historic Rococo period – a period in which upholstery was first developed, and when curved shapes and decorative detail became a hallmark – remains strong in France today. It heralded the idea of feminine comfort and introduced new ideas of comfort and fashion. This tradition was reflected in the colors and designs in the kitchen.

Many happy meals have been cooked and consumed in this kitchen, accompanied by some of the best wines Burgundy can produce. Despite the small space and limited amount of preparation area, the kitchen works well. Most of all you feel the kitchen belongs in its environment. The surroundings have merged into the inside of the building, bringing its indefinable qualities of time, magic, tradition and abundance inside.

emotional intelligence
a design that satisfies the heart

OPPOSITE The idea of home extends beyond the fabric of a building into one's emotional and family landscape. This kitchen adapts to the physical needs of each family member, depending on the dynamic of activity involved.

One of the most important needs a human being has as a precursor to a good life is a supportive emotional environment. By providing hard shelter, protection and the desire for nest building, how much can the physical environment contribute to a happy life? Can design improve, support or enhance an individual's emotional well-being?

Clues for us to work with are the way design can support agreeable behavior patterns within the four walls of a home. Stress, noise, lack of good communication, insufficient sunlight, lack of privacy and personal space, or poor attitudes to where we live and a sense of low status all damage equanimity. Bringing intelligence to emotion and expressing it in three-dimensional terms is quite a challenge. "Emotions are at the center of our aptitude for living", according to Daniel Goleman, author of the landmark book *Emotional Intelligence* which offers an alternative way of measuring intelligence. Goleman's thesis expounds that there is an applied intelligence that can make us excel and lead happy and well-balanced lives through the exercise of the rational mind and knowing oneself in enjoying the social arts, having the capacity for empathy with others and in harnessing passion. There are, he claims, many types of intelligence – from creative, musical, spatial and verbal to technical and intrapersonal – beyond those recognized by traditional IQ. His work has changed the way that people define intelligence, widening it to embrace a fuller and more comprehensive understanding of human spirit. Many of the intelligence skills he recognizes are those that are used when designing homes. In essence, emotional balance helps protect our health

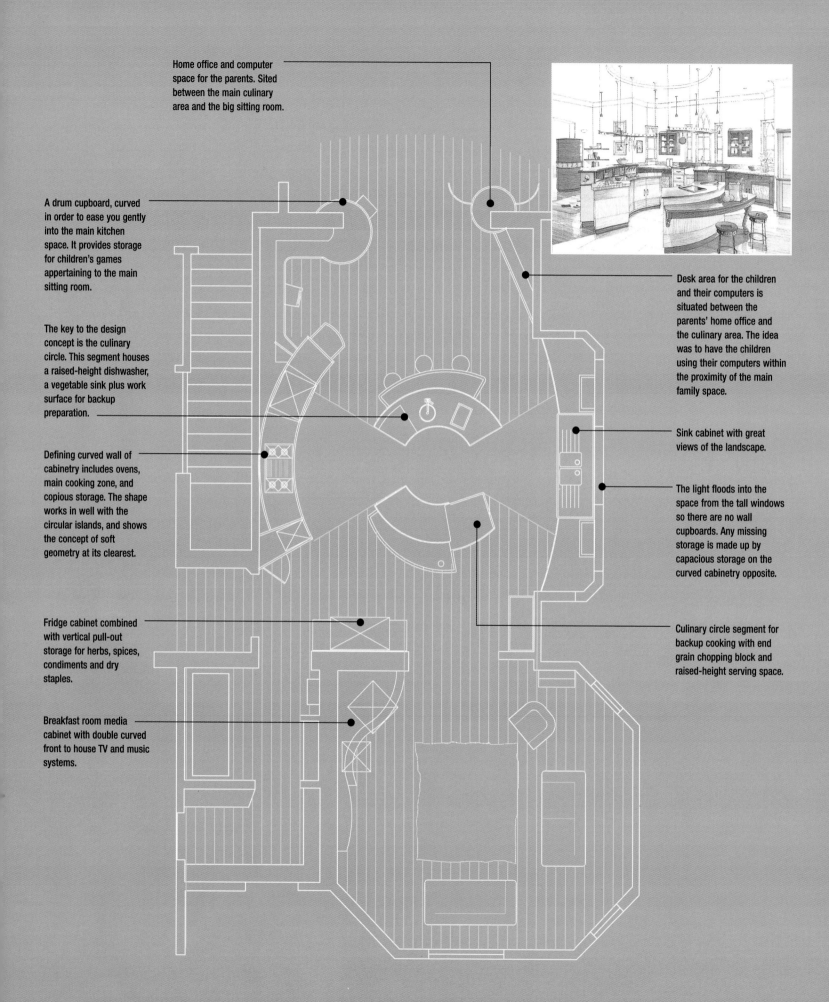

Home office and computer space for the parents. Sited between the main culinary area and the big sitting room.

A drum cupboard, curved in order to ease you gently into the main kitchen space. It provides storage for children's games appertaining to the main sitting room.

The key to the design concept is the culinary circle. This segment houses a raised-height dishwasher, a vegetable sink plus work surface for backup preparation.

Defining curved wall of cabinetry includes ovens, main cooking zone, and copious storage. The shape works in well with the circular islands, and shows the concept of soft geometry at its clearest.

Fridge cabinet combined with vertical pull-out storage for herbs, spices, condiments and dry staples.

Breakfast room media cabinet with double curved front to house TV and music systems.

Desk area for the children and their computers is situated between the parents' home office and the culinary area. The idea was to have the children using their computers within the proximity of the main family space.

Sink cabinet with great views of the landscape.

The light floods into the space from the tall windows so there are no wall cupboards. Any missing storage is made up by capacious storage on the curved cabinetry opposite.

Culinary circle segment for backup cooking with end grain chopping block and raised-height serving space.

Emotional intelligence of design is understanding how and what design does for us as individuals and society in general.

and well-being. Emotional intelligence of design is all about understanding how and what design can do in practical and emotional terms.

Design represents the thinking part of the process of making anything, from buildings to airplanes. It lays down the ground rules, the invention of a solution as well as its testing. For the design of interiors it begins with setting the scope of a project, sorting out needs and desires now and, if thought through properly, in the future also. What is key is applying emotional intelligence to the design process. A good brief sets up the infrastructure that will balance our

often complex emotional needs with those of the real world. Weaving our way through practical aspects like money, time scale and logistics and keeping our design vision in place needs considerable staying power and emotional direction; not yielding too much to distraction, but retaining a sense of delight and being fluid in our thinking is important to achieve new and effective solutions.

Karen and Ian began planning their new dream house in Virginia with a commitment to making it work for their young family of three children. They had realized that the kitchen was not just a place to cook, but a central place for active family life. There was no limitation placed on the amount of space available. The kitchen complex was to have the best views across the new home's landscape, and the proposal was to have a sitting room, a central culinary circle and a breakfast room as a series of consecutive spaces. The dilemma in building a new home is that ideas rapidly take on a solid unchangeable aspect once they get

ABOVE High ceilings with tall windows make the room feel spacious, and the scale of the furniture sits easily in the space – partly due to its curved shapes and easy sense of pedestrian flow.

LEFT The curved wall of cabinetry with its recessed ovens and copious storage represents the main cooking zone, the range being within easy reach.

PREVIOUS PAGES
LEFT Dramatic shapes produce a sense of order in the central island segment where the servery meets the preparation area.
RIGHT The pattern of fish swimming gives linear movement to the central island, suiting its curved shape, and provides an individual touch to the kitchen.

LEFT All the main cooking activities are contained in one area. The air extractor over the cooking zone contains a powerful but quiet system.

RIGHT View across the circular islands from the sitting room.

turned into three dimensions! To address this the skill of transporting ourselves into a future space before we get there is vital. We have to control our emotional feelings about how the décor will feel as well as how it will work. It's a more difficult task to get right than many realize. As in a prospective house purchase, we have to imagine ourselves there before we think of buying. We engage in emotional imagination to make sure it fits. We all find it hard to be flexible and have the faith to see a project through where there is a degree of the unknown, because by definition you are breaking new ground. Employing a designer who is experienced as a facilitator helps minimize the risk. There are two parts to his or her role. The first is to make the functional aspects work – dimensions, durability and body support – but the second is to achieve the emotional "feel good" factor. A space needs to welcome us in some way – raising our spirits to make us enjoy being there.

Karen was inspired by the idea of soft geometry. She appreciated the way it helped with the easy flow of people moving throughout the space even though there was plenty of it. She also liked the way the pure circular shape of a wraparound central island was symmetrical and created a natural focal point around which to establish a strong relationship between key kitchen furniture pieces. It linked up the sink to the main cooking wall and allowed for sociable cooking, with great sightlines into the whole suite of rooms. The key to the culinary circle was making all the kitchen activity a sociable process. Although the main cooking is done against the wall, there is a facility in the center if both Ian and Karen wish to cook at the same time. The space is

democratically used; that is, the furniture is evenly spread across the room, and its scale in a space of this size had to be complimentary. The surrounding storage cabinets are 8 feet tall in order to cope with the high ceilings and contain the central circle within their embrace.

All three children and two adults had their own work stations built into the design, each with computer terminals. A separate TV viewing area in the more intimately scaled breakfast room took some of the pressure off the sitting room end, which was reserved for family viewing. The family can coexist happily together in this open-plan kitchen. The excellent sightlines allow for conversation throughout while doing any activity from cooking to homework, playing with Lego or working on the computer.

The intelligence of any design is more than the sum of its parts. Being in a space is an emotional exercise. Movement through it, the quality of light and how it falls, the views out of the windows, the balance of materials, the color and finishes and décor, the different activity zones and the view lines across to adjacent rooms all are subliminally judged without reaching the conscious. The acid test is: Do people actually want to be in the space and do they spend time there voluntarily? In design there are always many different solutions. The intelligence is working out which one is best. There is rarely a straightforward route, so we need to engage all aspects of our intelligence to achieve the most comfortable and emotionally satisfying environment.

a question of taste
design as a matter of pleasure

For this client, it began at an early age, a childhood dream – the idea of building a house inspired by the children's adventure story, *Treasure Island,* by Robert Louis Stevenson. Many years later, the fantasy became reality, a cross between a palace and a barn, a place for hedonistic pursuits, for relaxation and entertaining. It was also an opportunity to defy the boundaries of good taste and homey interiors; for a self-made man with a great love of literature and trees, it represented a personal triumphant expression, a celebration of craftsmanship and bohemian ideas.

Many heritage homes and grand houses at the peak of 18th century good taste were considered to be of questionable taste when first built. Much Victorian architecture was of dubious taste, too. Think of the riot of ornamental woodwork, the clashing styles of buildings of any 19th-century city from San Francisco to Sydney, or Vienna with its Viennese Secession and art nouveau styles with its swirling floral over-indulgence, and ask where the idea of sobriety or good design manners had gone. These buildings and interiors are now accepted as buildings of intrinsic value. In comparative terms I hope that over time Highfield will be given a similar rating. It is not avant-garde, but I suspect most of those mentioned above weren't considered in that way either. They were more of an expression of an *arriviste* culture, part fashion, part exotic and full of personal or intimate meanings.

Felix Dennis, owner of Highfield, was unconcerned about other people's disapproval. He is a robust personality and enjoys a certain degree of controversy. From the planning through to the execution, he was involved in making detailed decisions about the building. The kitchen and dining area were positioned next to the open pool that formed the

LEFT Highfield's dining room and kitchen were inspired by *Treasure Island* by Robert Louis Stevenson. The client saw it as a remote island where you can make your own rules – an empire without grandeur, built with both function and with pleasure at its core, with the influence of the Caribbean climate and recycled boat elements as part of the theme.

Sink cabinet made from recycled pitch pine flanked by storage cupboards with scenes copied from Mervyn Peake's illustrations of *Treasure Island* on their façades.

Curved pantry wraps around the spiral staircase to the upstairs gallery. This provides much-needed storage, visual privacy and easy movement between kitchen and dining areas.

Rood screen with carvings depicting key scenes of the client's own life. It was designed to let light through from the pool area, but it also offers some privacy.

The circular island hints of clinker boat construction and easy geometry, and houses practical functions. The gantry above made with rope, hand-forged metalwork and pitch pine, built around the hand-adzed central pole employs the kind of materials that could have been found on Treasure Island.

The fridge and dumb waiter cabinet with copper panels and a large walnut cornice to hold the piece together display another illustration of Mervyn Peake's – of Admiral Benbow.

The bar and serving cupboard is a sumptuous piece of woodwork that reflects 17th-century high status furnituremaking, with rich use of veneers and ornament. A fine piece of furniture such as this might have been found in the captain's cabin.

A grand dining table with hand-carved pineapple legs and period carvers to match. Dining in sumptuous surroundings with echoes of history all around and great views out across the pool area make this a very unique setting in which to eat.

Fireplace with fender seat for relaxing after dinner.

focal point of the huge barnlike space – the main chamber of the building. The ambience of the interior was dominated by the large green oak barn structure that housed palm trees to convey a display of tropical opulence. The layout of the building had a kinship with a medieval church, a nave with side aisles or chapels. It allowed for smaller spaces to be created on the perimeter. Various elements such as a double oval-shaped swimming pool and spiral staircase brought unexpected but welcome interruptions to the building, allowing us to make unusually shaped spaces and elements of surprise. One of the best of these is arriving in the small entrance hall and seeing the entire building through a double-sided aquarium.

The décor in Highfield is not inspired by style but by story. It is at turns bizarre, amusing and occasionally, I hope, quite touching. There is a visible sense of freedom in the planning of the interior. In most house interiors there is a hierarchy of arrival and departure, defined areas of privacy and public use of space. At Highfield, these boundaries are blurred, and there is a random juxtaposition of private and functional space. These are spread around the eaves and edges of the cathedral-like plan. There are four walls, but the pool and its arbitrary shape, the lower height of the side aisles and particularly the spiral staircase mean the kitchen ends up in a corner – that is, partially hidden but attached through its open alliance with the dining room and its connection to the entrance area.

The absence of doors to demarcate rooms achieves a sense of easy movement and lingering, while still being in tune with the presence of other people in the building; for example, awareness of conversations in the seating area near the French doors draws you there. Someone swimming leads you to think about being in the pool. A person cooking brings you to the kitchen. Sociability is all, and accommodating that is the ultimate function of a leisure building. This echoes the new expanded role of the kitchen.

The kitchen here had no need of walls or doors. The whole space is heated, and air conditioned efficiently. Its allocation of space was adjacent to the pool, and the whole building was dedicated to entertainment. The traditional boundaries of a kitchen became blurred, yet there was still some need for some conventional planning associated with culinary activity. Preparation space, cooking, air ventilation, storage and refrigeration needed planning, as well as a food lift to the basement media room and games room, and to the library and bedrooms above.

LEFT Dining in style rather than reverence. How does one design for pleasure rather than just function? By addressing the senses – the mind, body and emotions. The mediums are color, texture, materials and shapes – the usual palette of a designer's oeuvre but expressed within a universe of design emotions.

BELOW The kitchen is practical although not recognizable as such, with so many bold references to a fantasy world of tall ships and swashbuckling crew!

I take up my pen in the year of grace 17—, and go back to
...ral Benbow' inn, and the brown old seaman, with th...

PREVIOUS PAGES:
LEFT View from the entrance hall into the kitchen. A plethora of exposed natural oak. The owner replanted two trees for every one felled to make the building.
RIGHT Hanging gantry for the kitchen island houses a riot of clanking hardware, jute ropes and wooden beams with concealed lights.

LEFT Apart from the willful enjoyment of designing something eye-catching, the island has an end grain chopping block and small vegetable sink for function as well as an open shelf for storage.

The spiral staircase inadvertently provided the perfect vehicle for planning a large storage cupboard around its perimeter to house all manner of kitchen equipment. It also gave the room a virtual wall.

With freedom from conventional domestic kitchen requirements, we had an opportunity to play and indulge in theatrics. Forms, materials, styles and function to an extent could be subverted and invested with imaginary elements. The circular island is constructed like a boat with a clinker-built hull that disappears into the floor; a mast in its center rises to a hanging rack packed with rigging; the cabinets around the sink have illustrations of *Treasure Island* characters painted on their façades; the curved patterned storage cupboard was inspired by reflections of moving water; in the banqueting hall the table stands on carved pineapples, the paneling is painted with faded patterns inspired by jewel shapes; the chandelier provides a medieval flavor with hand-patinated copper and

With freedom from conventional domestic kitchen requirements, we had an opportunity to play and indulge in theatrics.

complementary pineapples to match the table legs, and the rood screen has three carved panels that depict some of Felix's own life experiences.

None of these designs are rational in their formation or of good taste. They have a lighthearted quality, tactile and pleasantly offbeat. This seems to be closer to the spirit in which the castles, heritage homes and interiors of the past were built and that appears absent from so much of modern design.

The kitchen and dining spaces are within view of each other, but neither is compromised. The roguish element of strong and in some cases discordant individual pieces combines to make an atmosphere of being out of the ordinary. Perhaps interiors should enhance and connect to an inside life of the mind and not always be ruthlessly functional. Raising the spirits through whimsical and peculiar objects, furniture and design ideas can provide us with necessary relief from everyday life.

The energy released by working on such a project produced a satisfaction and pleasure that few other projects have managed. In lessons for other times, I think that giving the pleasure side more scope unleashes creativity and enthusiasm and produces an end result that continues to infect the building long after the makers and designers have left. The question of taste is transcended by pleasure.

In part, designing kitchens is about planning for social relations. Robert Louis Stevenson may be turning in his grave, but he has inspired a building planned for, albeit slightly unusual, social relations in the company of a theater of the senses. Not that we need to be too serious about all of this. The client enjoyed making a building of originality, the craftspeople sharpened their skills and the designers their pencils. Fantasies were indulged by all, and the many friends of the client get to enjoy using the building.

LEFT Slate between the end grain block makes an elegant use of materials. Extended handmade twisted metal handles for the drawer below make for easy opening.

MIDDLE Fiber-optic floor lights set in the mixed limestone checkered floor offer a useful addition to lighting effects. They change color and in the evenings add drama by picking up on the water-inspired pattern on the circular storage pantry.

BELOW The geometry of the curved pantry cupboard is a spiral, so as it narrows, the depth is right for a shelf. This has more fiber-optic lights incorporated and is ideal for serving drinks to take into the pool area beyond the dining room.

originality and self-expression
tailoring design to reflect individuality

OPPOSITE The client is a writer who has wide cultural interests, including Russian history. In this Manhattan brownstone, the kitchen replaced a first floor drawing room, and has embraced its former elegance by offering some unique design opportunities within.

The capacity for ferreting out the unexpected helps greatly with finding sources for originality and self-expression in interior design. To connect with your home, it is necessary to have the confidence to express your feelings, to engage with the world and enjoy its cultural offerings. I wonder sometimes whether it matters what people's enthusiasms are as long as they have them. Dullness is the bedfellow of an empty mind.

I have always been intrigued by independent-minded individuals. Many of the clients our studio attracts are in this category – they want something different, they know it must be there, but they can't find it through conventional kitchen companies. So much interior design, particularly in kitchens, tends to look the same and is a poor expression of their owner's life interests. These dissatisfied searchers need something more tailored to their individuality. It is not style they are after. It is more fundamental. When they arrive at our doorstep, we have a lively enthusiasm to tap into for an original but demanding design – a challenge that will happily have many hooks on which we can hang ideas. Such was the case here in this Manhattan brownstone, built in the early 20th century.

This was our second kitchen for the client. We had enjoyed working together in London on a small townhouse where we had pioneered some of my ideas about soft geometry. Here in New York we had more scope. Situated on the third floor within a suite of rooms, the kitchen was at the back; its tall ceiling and imposing marble fireplace gave the room a formality left over from grander times. There was no kitchen here before

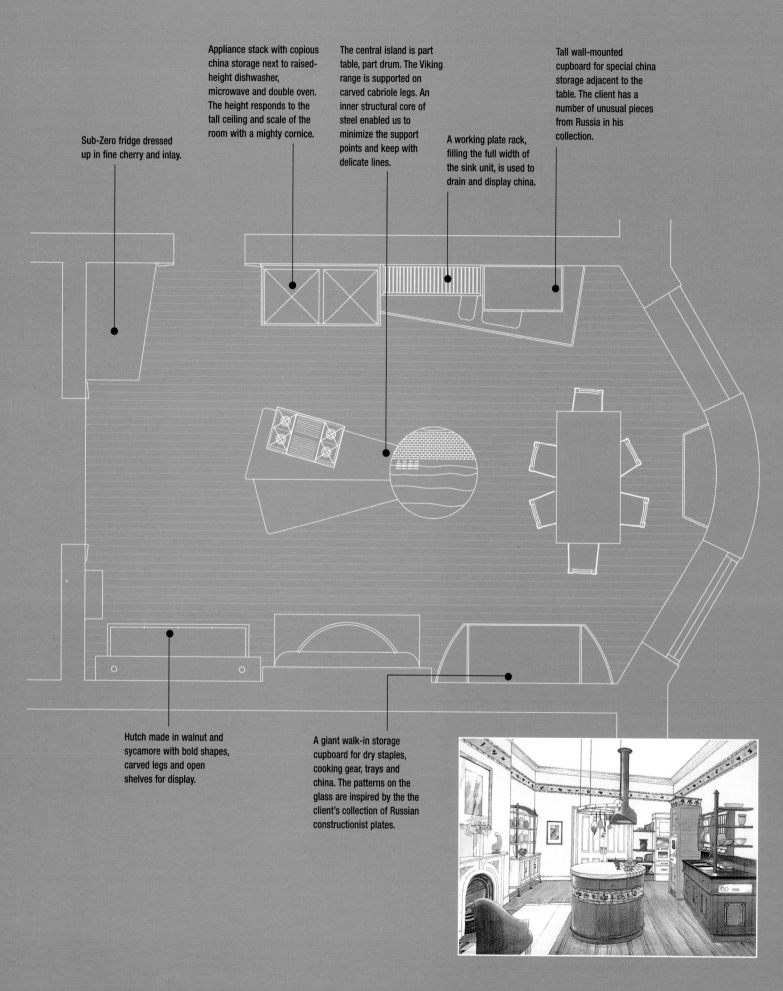

Sub-Zero fridge dressed up in fine cherry and inlay.

Appliance stack with copious china storage next to raised-height dishwasher, microwave and double oven. The height responds to the tall ceiling and scale of the room with a mighty cornice.

The central island is part table, part drum. The Viking range is supported on carved cabriole legs. An inner structural core of steel enabled us to minimize the support points and keep with delicate lines.

A working plate rack, filling the full width of the sink unit, is used to drain and display china.

Tall wall-mounted cupboard for special china storage adjacent to the table. The client has a number of unusual pieces from Russia in his collection.

Hutch made in walnut and sycamore with bold shapes, carved legs and open shelves for display.

A giant walk-in storage cupboard for dry staples, cooking gear, trays and china. The patterns on the glass are inspired by the the client's collection of Russian constructionist plates.

– it had been in the basement for staff only. There was no shortage of space as such, but as often is the case, there was a limited supply of wall space where more was required. We closed off a door to a landing and gained a pantry, which gave some extra storage, and then installed large pieces of free-standing furniture on either side of the chimney breast. The core of the design was the central island and the massive one-stop, high-service piece of furniture that acted as a sink cabinet, storage point and appliance housing, and housed two ovens, a microwave and a dishwasher.

One of the design hooks was the client's interest in Russia. He had seen the second "White Revolution" firsthand, when Yeltsin stood on a tank and saw off a military coup, allowing Gorbachev to return to power. He had been helping Russian friends in London with immigration problems and became intrigued with Russian culture. He started collecting Russian artifacts including

china dating from the constructivist period – the only modernist art movement allowed to flourish briefly after the Communist takeover.

How do you use influences to design and decorate your home so that they have a sense of appropriateness? They clearly come from your life experiences, but to what extent is an intellectual idea translatable? Should you plan out ideas or rely on touches of whimsy to provide no more than a light touch – a collection of accumulated, bustling mementoes, found items from flea markets and antique shops – to create your living environment? I suspect this might be fine in living rooms, but there is a different challenge in kitchens because the architecture needs to be taken into account and numerous cabinets need to be constructed for task-specific functions. They make such a major impact, you have to consider their aesthetic quality. If you don't, they can become awkward, ugly boxes that, while serving a function, give no pleasure. They will

BELOW Grouped together as a four-in-one combined sink cabinet, plate rack, condiment cupboard and appliance stack assemblage. This is a furnishing technique we use to cope with large rooms where scale is an issue. The pattern painted on the cornice is inspired by Russian Cossack art and is boldly executed with giant ribbons.

To connect with your home, it is necessary to have the confidence to express your feelings, to engage with the world and enjoy its cultural offerings.

RIGHT Bouncing light off a rich variety of work surface materials, individual shapes, patterns and objects from different countries make for an original design that expresses the owner's broad cultural interests.

LEFT The tradition of fine furniture craft is harnessed by the use of sensual shapes, rich textures and pattern. The painted band on the drum is adapted from Russian constructivist period plates.

BELOW The top of the hutch has a curved roof plank that acts as cornice and frame and is held in position with yacht hardware.

RIGHT The range is supported on hand carved cabriole legs with gold leaf buttons. Being open underneath gives a spacious quality to the room and accommodates your feet much better without the presence of a plinth.

undermine everything else you do in the space. This is the core issue with kitchen design – employing a large number of new cabinets to be highly functional and visually and emotionally pleasing at the same time. Incorporating some of one's life experiences seems a perfectly good way to start, although perhaps not to finish. Over-themed environments are tedious and absurd. The Russian constructivist pattern was kept to the artwork on the drum and the pantry cupboard, where it provided a striking focus for the large pieces of cabinetry and the use of Russian Cyrillic lettering was painted as a frieze around the walls at high level. You don't feel you are in Russia, but you have a sense of foreignness – loosely there and providing some echo of another time and place.

We chose American cherry in a simple paneled construction for the basic style of the cabinetry, traditionally made with little embellishment. Since the scale of the room was so large, we formed a group of cabinets as a single entity, which comprised the sink functions, appliances and some storage pertaining to washing and cooking. With this and the island carrying the main active culinary functions, we could spread out other requirements across the room. All the furniture is scaled up in size to fit in with the height and grandeur of the room.

The multilevel island radiates out from a large food preparation drum in the shape of a grand piano. Hovering above is a giant stainless steel boat-shaped canopy to house the commercial air extractor. The Viking cooktop ensconced in the middle of the upper level work surface is supported on carved legs with hints of Sheraton Colonial influence. These celebrate the exuberant pleasures of a person who loves the magic of history and a designer playing with craftsmanship's ability to recall it. As homeowners we make our own imaginary history for ourselves when we create our own room sets. We carry our own personal architecture experiences in our heads, too, that we can raid when we need ideas.

The richness of other times and places gives resonance to material objects that raises their value beyond just material things. Perhaps that's one of the main reasons behind what we are doing when we decorate our homes and design our kitchens. There is a bohemian trying to get out when we start to design truly individual spaces for ourselves.

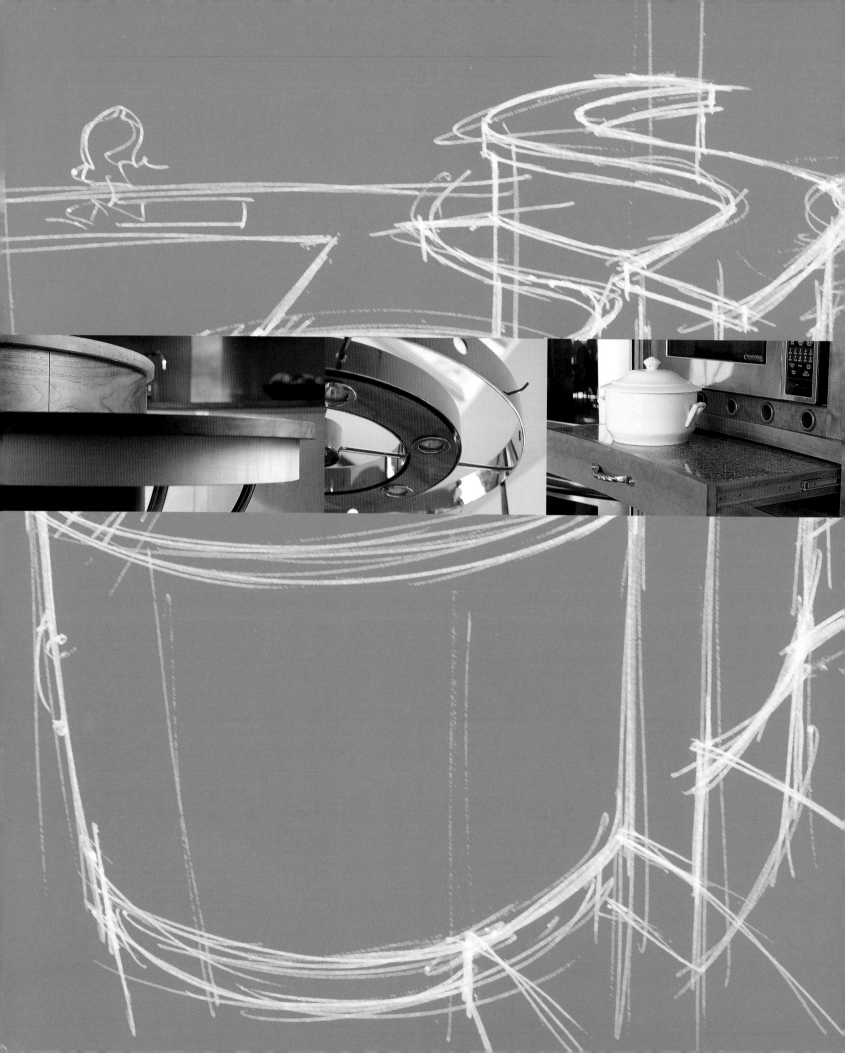

kitchen works: design analysis

Bridging the gap between ideas and reality is the focus of this chapter, providing techniques to translate the ideas from the design stories of previous chapters into reality, in the context of your own kitchen environment. Useful advice on applying design thinking to your own spaces, covering such diverse areas as body ergonomics, design for cooking, basic measurements, countertop lore, work surface materials, and paint and pattern. Raw data on some of the key ideas that I have been researching for the last 20 years offer a new, if unconventional, viewpoint including designing with furniture as opposed to long rows of base and wall cabinets, and how to configure the different shapes and uses for a central island. Use this section to take ideas one step closer to making your kitchen thoughts a reality.

creating the design

Design is a conversation, so it is important to keep it as fluid as possible for as long as necessary – until you are happy with the end result. Consider some key questions in relation to your kitchen design plans – Have you decided on the key functions of the space? Will it be a sociable kitchen, open plan, have dining facilities? What are the uses of the surrounding rooms that will affect what you do in the new kitchen space? Assuming you have read much from the preceding chapters and carried out some early design exercises on paper, you should be able to discern whether you can place your key items in the space, and what should be their approximate scale. Until some investigation with a floor plan is carried out, opportunities to maximize worktop space, or to fit in a couch, or decide upon the size of cabinets will have to wait. The more marginal requirements remain up in the air – for example, whether or not to go for a central island, whether or not there is enough room for a walk-in pantry or what specific architectural alterations would enhance the space. It is the bigger decisions that need to be addressed initially.

When I first go into the space chosen to make a kitchen, many thoughts are darting around my head. My antennae are picking up clues, from observations about the clients' personal taste to the style of the architecture. At this stage the new kitchen does not exist; its space is the space in the mind. The end result will be due to careful analysis of ergonomics and verifiable phenomena. But what about the other parts – the creative difference expected from a good design and the qualities associated with it, such as delight, visual harmony, and sense of comfort and belonging? How can you make the space sing a little, make it different, unique and yet appealing without it seeming self-conscious? Working up the design for your kitchen requires a pragmatic and organized approach.

It is worth remembering there are always many solutions to the same problem, different designs for the same space. They will have different emphasis, gains, and disadvantages for certain aspects. They may not be better or worse, just different. I often say to clients if you are getting 75 percent of what you want, you are doing rather well! You rarely end up getting everything. And learning to say no to some things means more clarity, and may even result in your saying yes to bigger things that may emerge later.

Try to leave at least two corners free, as they define the architecture. This 30-inch high wall-hung corner cabinet for a TV leaves the corner visible, particularly at the floor and ceiling, and is a good compromise.

Two steps down to the kitchen means the eating area is separate but within easy eye contact of the cook. It also means the floor finish can be softer or different.

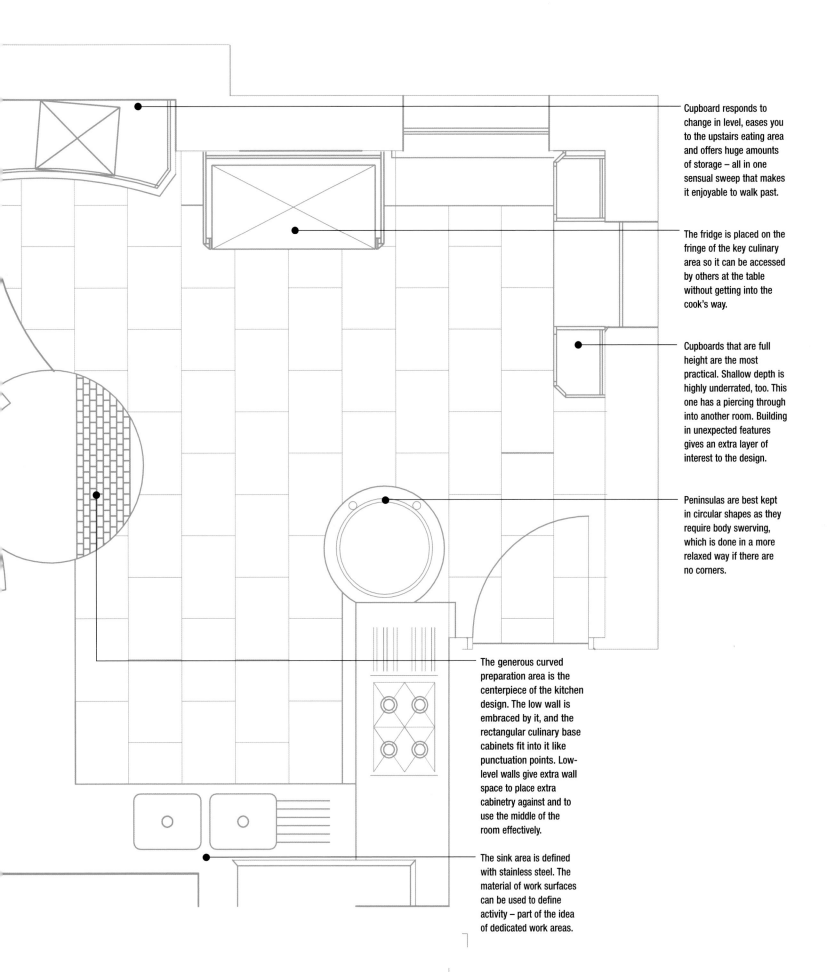

Cupboard responds to change in level, eases you to the upstairs eating area and offers huge amounts of storage – all in one sensual sweep that makes it enjoyable to walk past.

The fridge is placed on the fringe of the key culinary area so it can be accessed by others at the table without getting into the cook's way.

Cupboards that are full height are the most practical. Shallow depth is highly underrated, too. This one has a piercing through into another room. Building in unexpected features gives an extra layer of interest to the design.

Peninsulas are best kept in circular shapes as they require body swerving, which is done in a more relaxed way if there are no corners.

The generous curved preparation area is the centerpiece of the kitchen design. The low wall is embraced by it, and the rectangular culinary base cabinets fit into it like punctuation points. Low-level walls give extra wall space to place extra cabinetry against and to use the middle of the room effectively.

The sink area is defined with stainless steel. The material of work surfaces can be used to define activity – part of the idea of dedicated work areas.

lore of basic measurements

Throughout the book, each kitchen is accompanied by a plan. This helps explain the way the kitchen works, while the photographs represent a visual collage with which to comprehend the design. Designing a kitchen starts with developing a floor plan. The footprint is the vehicle by which we generate and communicate the ideas. Understanding plans is essential for discussing interior design, hence the emphasis on plans in this book.

Over the last decade kitchens may have expanded in the amount of space devoted to them, but the additional space is being devoted to sociable activities. The amount of space available for culinary activity has remained constant. There is nearly always too much demand in the core area, too much to fit into the area that is available. Tightly controlled planning and sequencing of tasks is therefore essential. By setting out dedicated work areas we can minimize waste of space. Planning for countertop space per se is a poor way of designing.

This section deals with minimum, ideal and maximum dimensions for key aspects of kitchen planning. The diagrams shown in this chapter provide some key ergonomic dimensions.

ABOVE When designing a comfortable home space, respect simple laws of scale and carefully consider the individual character of each piece of furniture to achieve a compatibility of style, color, shape and space. Avoid overcrowding and encourage visual pleasure through variety and natural materials.

RIGHT Expression of free-standing pieces is still achievable even when a run of cabinets is best conjoined. Avoid placing wall cabinets above active work surfaces as they interfere at eye level.

BASIC KITCHEN DIMENSIONS

Establish the natural routes across the room between furniture, exits and entrances. Identify the old working triangle within this (cooktop, sink and preparation area). Draw lines between these to establish key movement patterns, and design the furniture to avoid coming too far outside the lines.

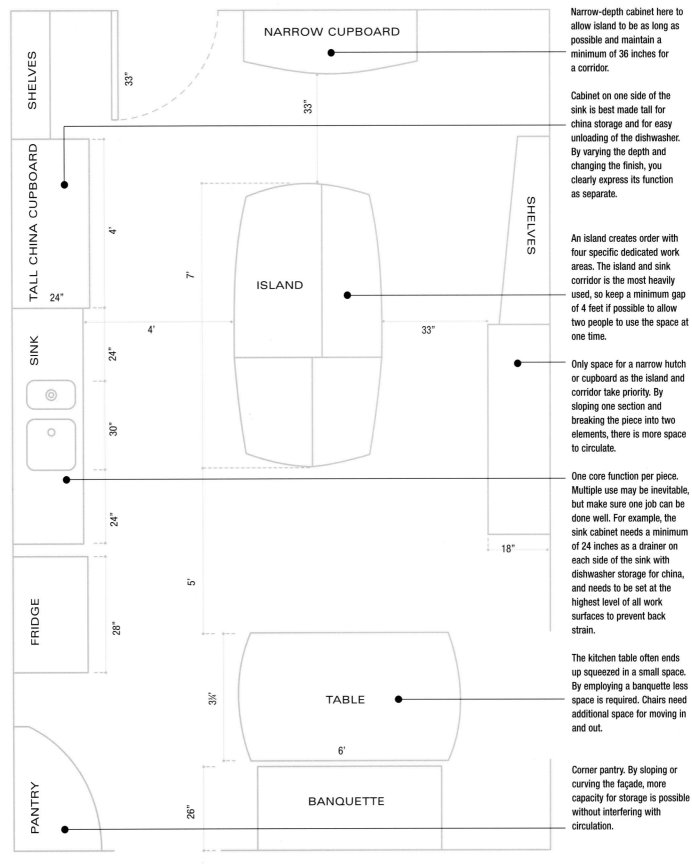

Narrow-depth cabinet here to allow island to be as long as possible and maintain a minimum of 36 inches for a corridor.

Cabinet on one side of the sink is best made tall for china storage and for easy unloading of the dishwasher. By varying the depth and changing the finish, you clearly express its function as separate.

An island creates order with four specific dedicated work areas. The island and sink corridor is the most heavily used, so keep a minimum gap of 4 feet if possible to allow two people to use the space at one time.

Only space for a narrow hutch or cupboard as the island and corridor take priority. By sloping one section and breaking the piece into two elements, there is more space to circulate.

One core function per piece. Multiple use may be inevitable, but make sure one job can be done well. For example, the sink cabinet needs a minimum of 24 inches as a drainer on each side of the sink with dishwasher storage for china, and needs to be set at the highest level of all work surfaces to prevent back strain.

The kitchen table often ends up squeezed in a small space. By employing a banquette less space is required. Chairs need additional space for moving in and out.

Corner pantry. By sloping or curving the façade, more capacity for storage is possible without interfering with circulation.

COUNTER HEIGHTS

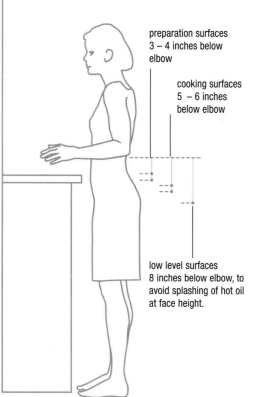

preparation surfaces
3 – 4 inches below
elbow

cooking surfaces
5 – 6 inches
below elbow

low level surfaces
8 inches below elbow, to
avoid splashing of hot oil
at face height.

SINK HEIGHT

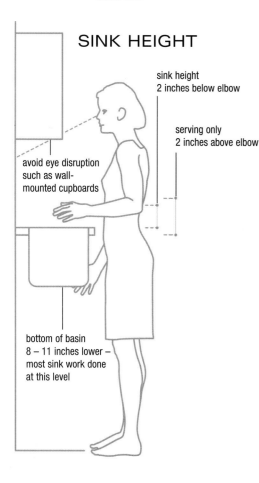

sink height
2 inches below elbow

serving only
2 inches above elbow

avoid eye disruption
such as wall-
mounted cupboards

bottom of basin
8 – 11 inches lower –
most sink work done
at this level

body ergonomics

The needs of the body – its sensual and physical accommodation in interior design – have been catered to, even while the basic design criteria are often addressed. I was taught the Alexander Technique after I became ill during the early part of my career and needed to address poor body physique. It taught me how to move with a sense of economy and become aware of how much this affects the way you use and experience furniture, work at practical tasks as well as move around space. Here I have listed some key body-friendly design measurements. I was also influenced by *Coming to Our Senses* by Morris Berman who wrote about how we have literally lost our senses, not our minds – but our bodies – and how we are denied our physicality in Western culture.

An understanding of how to support the human body is vital to good kitchen design. Body ergonomics originally started with industrial studies of making factories more efficient, but they are of value in making domestic tasks easier. The body performs more effectively with an economy of movement. Keep to familiar work patterns where possible. Efficient design creates a sense of order that makes for more relaxed and productive cooking as well as other kitchen tasks. Relaxing the other parts of your body will makes your energy go farther.

FAR LEFT TOP The spine should be kept straight, bending from the hips, not the neck. Counter heights should accommodate that.

FAR LEFT The less the amount of movement, the more time saved for preparation. Washing needs the highest work surface height since the floor of the basin is much lower, approximately 2 inches.

LEFT The cooktop is an area that needs ergonomic attention because of safety issues. Simple rules of thumb suggest heatproof surfaces up to a minimum of 16 inches are needed to prevent fat from being splashed onto the walls or work surface behind.

RIGHT Using different heights for dedicated work surfaces defines these areas in ergonomic terms, contributing practically and aesthetically to the kitchen's whole.

BELOW Furniture, storage, and work surfaces need to support the height and dimensions of the human body. Our key measurements are taken from clients' flexed elbow height. For example, preparing food needs to be done on a surface 3 inches below.

OVEN SAFETY

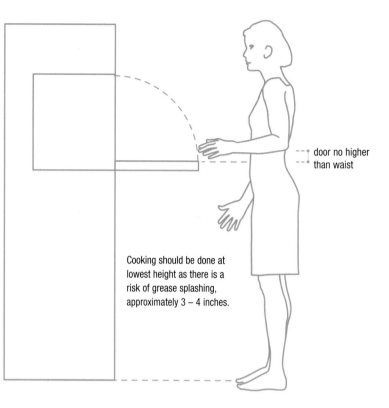

door no higher than waist

Cooking should be done at lowest height as there is a risk of grease splashing, approximately 3 – 4 inches.

CUPBOARD ACCESS

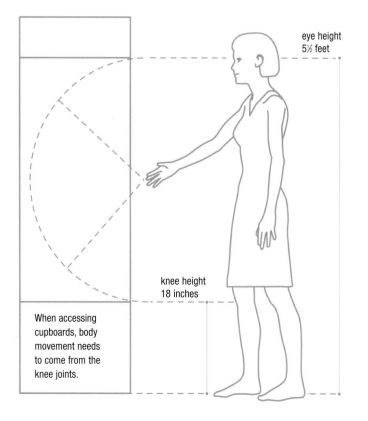

eye height 5½ feet

knee height 18 inches

When accessing cupboards, body movement needs to come from the knee joints.

intelligent heights

The following guidelines should be considered when moving around your personal kitchen space. Whether it is reaching for stored cupboard ingredients, standing at a worktop or washing up, each task demands a set of mindful body mechanics and good design to help provide maximum comfort and avoidance of injury.

when accessing a cupboard, movement should come from the knee joints. Keep the spine straight, bend from the hips, not the neck. Avoid regularly used storage below knee height to minimize bending down repeatedly.

furniture, storage and work surfaces need to support the height and dimensions of the human body. The key measurements in our design are taken from clients' flexed elbow height (FE). For example, preparing food needs to be done on a surface 3 inches below FE. Dishwashing needs the highest work surface height as the floor of the basin is much lower, approximately 2 inches FE, while cooking should be done at the lowest height, as there is a risk of fat splashing—approximately 3 – 4 inches.

OPPOSITE Heatproof surfaces and parking points nearby should be a minimum of 14 inches, allowing you to take a large pan off the stove in a hurry.

TOP RIGHT AND RIGHT Consider what tools and equipment you need immediately at hand when cooking, and think about whether you need a dedicated piece of furniture for it. Using the lore of basic measurements, calculate the best heights and means of access that allow for efficient movement.

STORAGE ACCESS

poor access area

most useful height
3½ – 4 feet

eye height
5 – 5½ feet

arm radius
24 – 32 inches

knee height
18 – 20 inches

poor access area

ABOVE The height of furniture that is not part of the immediate culinary area should still complement the height rationale of the overall design, and should not be compromised.

FAR LEFT Appliance storage units are cabinets with either fold-back doors or tambour fronts where you can store and use appliances in situ. The appliances can be permanently plugged in. Without doors taking up valuable space or preventing access, you effectively have more work surface.

By designing key storage areas to the best possible heights, movement becomes automatic, and this helps to fulfill the comfort of cooking.

body ergonomics **135**

RIGHT Personal configuration of needs. This stone top with vegetable sink is carved out of one piece of stone and doubles up in use for tea and coffee making. Its curved shape allows full access to the Aga nearby and has the semblance of being like a console table in a hallway, being both useful and elegant.

LEFT Worktop material defines use. End grain hardwood provides the best surface for cutting on, while the granite immediately adjacent is waterproof and dense, so is ideal for use around a cooking zone. The flow is efficient between them with its gently curved shape.

IDEAL COUNTERTOP DIMENSIONS

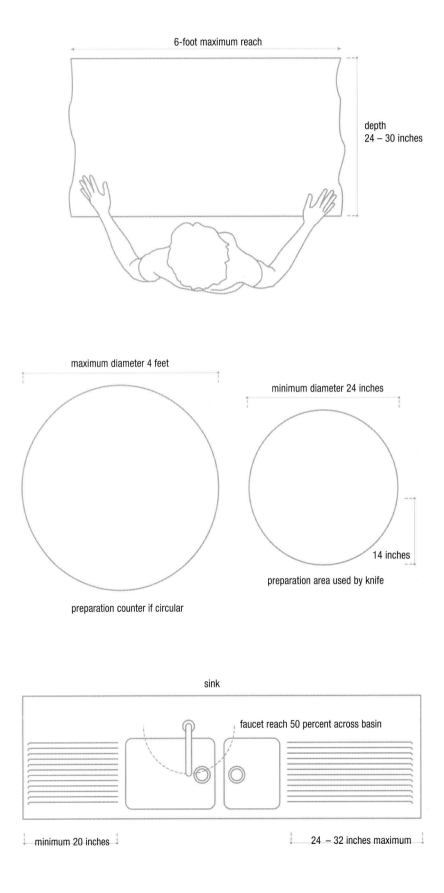

6-foot maximum reach

depth
24 – 30 inches

maximum diameter 4 feet

preparation counter if circular

minimum diameter 24 inches

14 inches

preparation area used by knife

sink

faucet reach 50 percent across basin

minimum 20 inches

24 – 32 inches maximum

countertop lore

The choice of surfaces in kitchen design is one of the main ways of defining activity. The best kitchens work if there is a clear sense of order, a hierarchy of needs sequenced for their height, proximity and surface area, to assist with the cooking process, sociability and flow of people using the kitchen together at any one time. Too much preparation area can distance the sink too far from the cooking zone, so don't oversize any activity; if you do, the excess space will end up as shelves anyway. Early in my design career, I developed the concept of dedicated work areas, which allows you to design one piece of furniture to cover one activity well. If you always go to the same place to chop on the end grain block, you naturally cluster the tools around it for food preparation, and generally move around the kitchen without extraneous effort.

The surface material itself is the final arbiter of activity. The inherent properties such as density, porosity, durability, as well as your personal preferences for color or grain configuration, inform you of their suitability. Whatever surface you use will have advantages and disadvantages. Details of a variety of surfaces are given on page 157.

design for cooking

There are many kitchens that are designed without real thought for the cook. Here is some advice to make the process of cooking more practical as well as enjoyable:

avoid long distances between cooking, washing and preparation. If they become too long, consider shortening work surfaces or doubling up some of the activities. For example, have two dishwashing areas – one for the cooking activity and one for table-related dishes, glasses and so on. The latter one could be placed nearer the table and be backed up with a second dishwasher, which is useful if you are feeding more than eight people.

dedicated work areas allow you to create a strong sense of order by carrying out specific tasks in one place without the need for excessive space. This allows you to reinforce what you can do in each place more precisely, thereby tightening up your priorities between each task area. This can be achieved without creating an obtrusive impact on the appearance of the kitchen and links well with the idea of having free-

standing furniture to carry out each task. It provides a sense of hidden organization.

- Alternate high and low use areas. If two people want to cook it is very helpful, but also in intensively used or kitchens where space is at a premium, plan enough space between cooking and preparation areas so you can set down hot pans around the cooktop and receptacles for putting different prepared foods as you sequence the cutting and chopping processes.
- Low level areas for specific functions, pastrymaking and bread kneading is vital for dough enthusiasts, preferably designed with a hard, inert and cold surface. It needs to be low to get your body weight over the rolling pin or when you knead the dough.

democratic planning – that is, planning activity to be evenly spread throughout the space. If you have one area of the kitchen being used intensely and then large areas where little is happening, something may be amiss. You can't always get an even intensity of use but aim for democratic use of the space for each activity. Make the

IDEAL DISTANCES FOR COOKING DYNAMICS

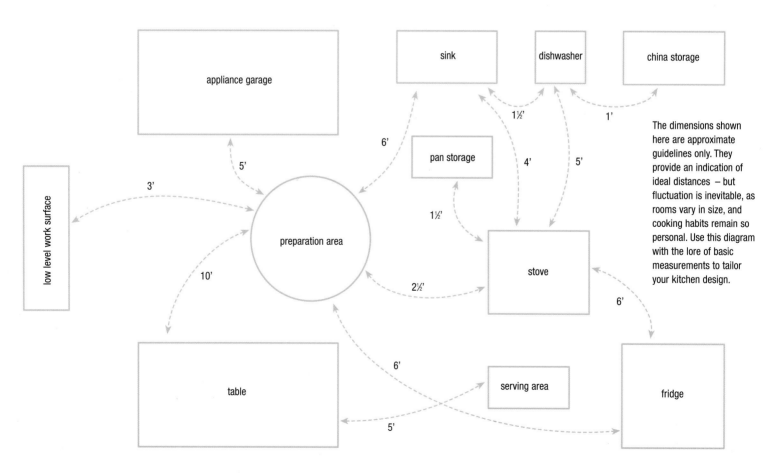

The dimensions shown here are approximate guidelines only. They provide an indication of ideal distances – but fluctuation is inevitable, as rooms vary in size, and cooking habits remain so personal. Use this diagram with the lore of basic measurements to tailor your kitchen design.

FAR LEFT "Parking space" made from a heat-friendly surface is essential for space efficiency. Here the use of a lid to cover a less regularly used cooktop creates extra parking space when not in use.

LEFT In places where there is no immediate empty surface or a fold-down oven front is not being used, a pull-out surface with a masonry insert is a sound safety feature.

BELOW A quiet ventilator/extractor fan for cooking fumes is vital, otherwise you won't turn it on except on rare occasions. Placing the fan inside the flue helps to reduce the noise.

kitchen a sociable place; one of the best ways of doing this is to face into the room while you are prepping and cooking.

vary your storage options

Different tools and equipment are best stored in different formats – open, closed, narrow, deep, tall or hanging. Vessels such as pottery or cast iron and stainless ware look attractive on display, adding atmosphere and visual appeal to the space. Small utensils hung from a gantry right next to the prep or cooking point are accessible and ready for action without bending down.

good tools of the cook

Make sure you have the right tools at hand in drawers below, adjacent to, or hanging from the gantry above your cooking area. Check the efficiency of lighting in the main preparation areas. Correct lighting conditions require there to be no shadows in front of you while prepping or cooking. If you have a special style of cooking, make a list of tools you need for it and think about whether you need a dedicated piece of furniture for it. For example, if you use a lot of spices or herbs, you need a shallow cupboard or drawer for storing them close at hand.

and for good measure

At the start of the project, make a checklist to see if you have covered all your requirements. If you have achieved 75 percent of what you asked for and in the right configurations, the kitchen will be very serviceable and user friendly.

soft geometry

Soft geometry is a key philosophy for planning our kitchens. In essence, it is the use of curved shapes qualified by the application of ergonomics, complementing how the human body moves through interior space, and how we use and support it in appropriate ways. Most kitchens are unsympathetic to the needs of the human body, often ignoring the basic reality that we don't walk in straight lines. Soft geometry offers more flow, making the easiest journey between two points.

in contemporary architecture
complex buildings are being constructed with revolutionary geometry. Computer modeling allows designers to create forms that are more naturalistic, making buildings more like sculptures. The shapes Frank Gehry uses in the Guggenheim Museum in Bilbao and Walt Disney Concert Hall in Los Angeles reveal

ABOVE Curved work surfaces still gain from recessed cupboards below so that your feet can be accommodated underneath without having to be forced sideways or awkwardly positioned.

RIGHT Curved shapes, especially in the middle of the room, are much easier to react with. The body needs to focus less on movement. Peripheral vision uses up a surprising amount of mental activity.

NARROW KITCHEN

RIGHT Where space is at a premium, for example, in this narrow kitchen, curved counters provide a more effective sequencing of tasks as well as more efficient movement of people in the space at the same time.

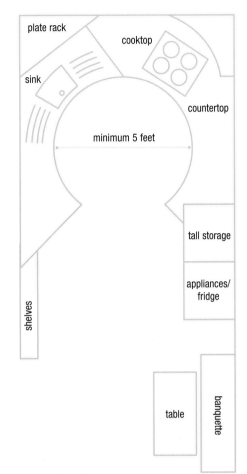

plate rack

cooktop

sink

countertop

minimum 5 feet

tall storage

appliances/ fridge

shelves

table

banquette

PARALLEL CORRIDORS

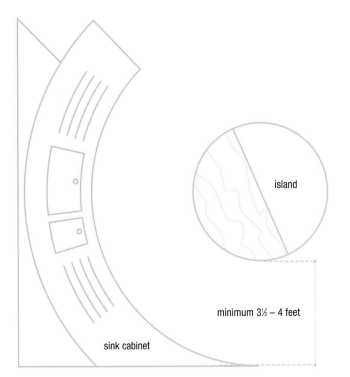

island

minimum 3½ – 4 feet

sink cabinet

WEDGE-SHAPED FLOOR

RIGHT Around doorways or where maximum cabinet capacity is required at thresholds between rooms, wedge-shaped furniture is a design-friendly way to achieve good movement.

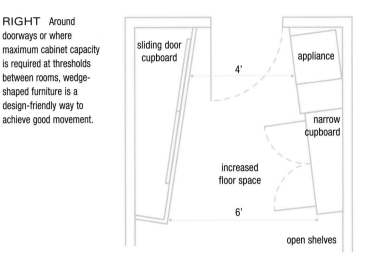

sliding door cupboard

4'

appliance

narrow cupboard

increased floor space

6'

open shelves

complex indoor and outdoor spaces that are more organic and hardly refer to the conventions of rectilinear architecture. The boundaries for furniture design and interior spaces have been extended. We have new opportunities to make our homes comfortable and humane spaces.

a curved shape is not in principle any better than round. The lessons of classical architecture show how to use circular shapes sparingly, particularly when applied to bow-fronted houses or as the centerpiece for a long, flat façade, to add modeling or focus. Today curves are used to play, distort or surprise in a more radical way. The enjoyment is in the uniqueness or individuality of the shapes rather than their formality and predictability. Balanced asymmetry offers an interesting way forward, but there are limits. Most people don't want to live in weirdly-shaped interiors or in houses that are widely organic in shape. Rectangular-shaped rooms are reassuringly normal and predictable, but softening the inner fabric or the furniture for ease of use and gentle movements is a fortuitous balance.

we move about easier when there is space, light, no sharp corners and an order in our interior layout planning. The sharp corners on a rectangular central island even at hip level send out messages "treat me with care." Rounded edges or, better still, long, oval shapes, create a more relaxed form of movement and discard the need to steer ourselves into a particular position for preparation. We can also share the work surface with a partner, as opposed to being squeezed into using a constricted length of façade.

LEFT When island and counter are parallel, the flow is pleasurable, and the sequencing linear and progressive.

LEFT Hanging gantries usually follow the lines of the furniture below. Their main function is for housing lighting above the preparation area and for keeping small utensils within easy reach.

BELOW LEFT Deep curved saucepan drawers benefit from the seamless row of long handles that offer easy gripping and accentuate the pleasing arc.

BELOW RIGHT Drainer grooves follow the outside curved edge of the stone sink surface.

ABOVE LEFT Narrow strips of glass butted up together form a faceted front that can be used in curved doors if you do not want to go to the trouble of commissioning specially curved glass.

ABOVE RIGHT Turned leg with handmade globe decoration gives a whimsical touch.

RIGHT Curved walls double as preparation zones and define eating areas – with good sightlines from the cooking area to the sociable areas.

RIGHT The furniture forms the geometry. Here this multipurpose giant cupboard also leads you through a change in level.

soft geometry details

Key aspects of planning for soft geometry:

create an easy flow of movement throughout the space so that obstacles feel they belong rather than impose. Imagine that a river has been flowing through the space and over time the water has ground away all protrusions. The river makes its pathway easy flowing.

design central pieces with rounded edges, particularly central islands and peninsulas. This makes for easier use between the work surfaces, too.

at pinch points where distances between the cabinetry is tight, create soft shapes that allow for smaller corridors, allowing the user to make bigger work surfaces when space is limited.

avoid always using the walls to position the cabinetry. Think of the focus as the center of the space so people using the kitchen are able to look around the room, not at the walls. This is more sociable, and makes better use of the room.

as a design exercise imagine yourself moving around as if you were partially sighted. This helps you decide how easy it is to move around the furniture without being injured or disrupted.

be aware of the role of peripheral vision; what happens at the corner of our vision surprisingly uses up a lot of mental activity. The lack of sharp edges makes for more relaxed movement.

use curves, which add a soft, sensual quality to the design, but don't employ them everywhere. They work best when there is a functional purpose to their deployment.

island analysis

Central islands offer the best means for facing into the room while preparing and cooking. The sociable period of any meal is during its preparation, and therefore eye contact with others in the room at that moment is desirable. Visual access to entrance doors and keeping an eye on children are facilitated by looking across the room, not at the wall.

There are two key planning advantages. The island is often the ideal link piece between two cabinet runs that spring out of a corner, forming a working triangle. They also create efficient parallel work areas – a wall-based sink cabinet – reinforcing the activities of each.

A limitation on the use of islands is the width of the room. If the room is 16 feet wide there will be tight circulation and it may be better to go for a peninsula, saving the circulation space required for two pathways. Soft geometry gives us more flexibility, both to create different sized work areas and also to squeeze more surface at points where rectangular geometry would be too disruptive.

RIGHT This enclosed island is expressed as a linear sequence of surfaces, each defining a dedicated use that allows the cook to face into the center of the space.

A walk-in island is the most sociable of all configurations – whenever you look up from the task you are performing, you have potential eye contact with a person or a view.

WALK-IN ISLAND

11'

36"

4½'

33"

9'

raised dishwasher

counter/storage

storage

CENTRAL ISLAND ANALYSIS

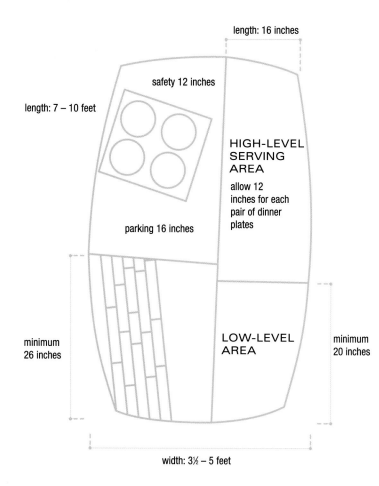

length: 16 inches

length: 7 – 10 feet

safety 12 inches

HIGH-LEVEL SERVING AREA

allow 12 inches for each pair of dinner plates

parking 16 inches

minimum 26 inches

LOW-LEVEL AREA

minimum 20 inches

width: 3½ – 5 feet

LEFT The island becomes a kit of parts rather than a formal piece of furniture. It draws the focus of culinary activities away from the convention of wall based worktops and into the centre of the kitchen.

This multi-purpose, split-level island serves every culinary task, with its efficient use of worktop area and storage capacity below. A number of task-oriented combinations will work, according to the anticipated frequency of culinary activity; for example, the addition of a small sink in the island makes all the difference if prepping food on a daily basis.

BELOW The island represents one of the best ways of organising kitchen activity to your own requirements. Here in four versions you can see that different dimensions, shapes and functions create extremely flexible and well tailored end results. The soft geometry makes them easier to move around as well as to use.

The key to designing islands is to have a clear sense of order. Dedicated work areas, with each function being catered to, both minimum and maximum sizes, provide sensible space for cooking, prepping, parking, serving, breakfast bar requirements or low-level areas for small appliances and pastrymaking. This helps make the island a hardworking and effective center for culinary activity. Absurdly long countertops distort kitchen design and reduce the opportunity for additional furniture pieces and create unnecessarily long walking between fringe or secondary functions such as using fridges, storage or the table.

Storage underneath is configured according to individual needs. A common request is for pan storage directly underneath the cooktop. Also, a built-in trash can close to the preparation area allows economy of movement, while a chopping block with a waste chute below allows for recycling waste. It is good to avoid solid blocks of furniture and instead, follow the sequence of the dedicated work surfaces and have some open space below, especially on the nonworking side. This can have unexpected uses, such as temporary shopping bag placement, a place for a dog to sleep out of harm's way or even a spot for small children to make temporary dens.

ISLAND SHAPES

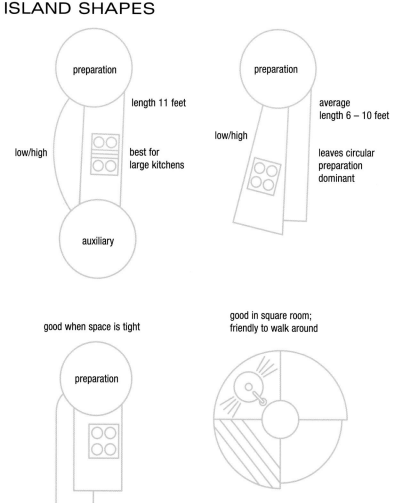

preparation

length 11 feet

low/high

best for large kitchens

auxiliary

good when space is tight

preparation

average length 6 – 10 feet

low/high

leaves circular preparation dominant

good in square room; friendly to walk around

preparation

average diameter 6 feet

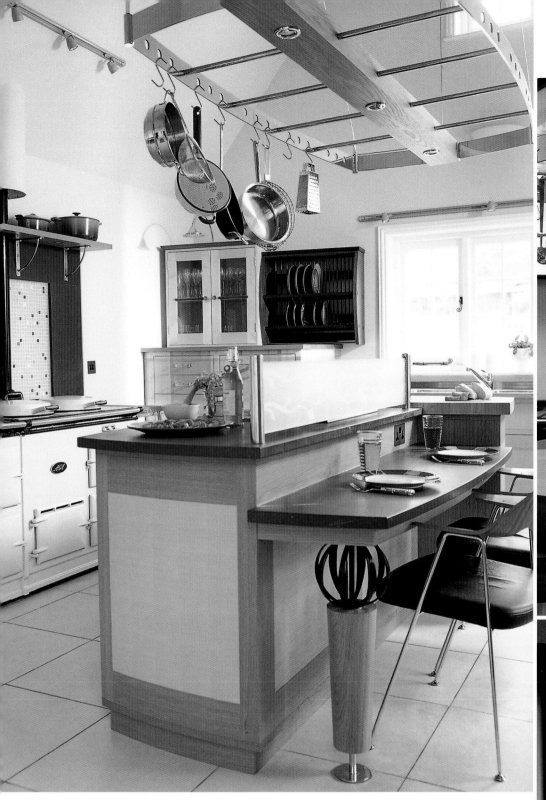

ABOVE Islands have a more focused working arrangement if the surface is divided into dedicated work areas – here there is a backup cooking zone, a preparation end grain wood surface, and a low-level area for general parking that also provides a place for people to sit.

TOP RIGHT The curved end on this island is a good size for preparation; one half has end grain block for preparation and the other doubles as a serving area and backup preparation table.

RIGHT The width, length and construction of this low-level area is more like a table that happens to be adjacent. The island becomes like a kit of parts rather than a formal piece of furniture.

cabinetry and inlay

OPPOSITE 1960s inspired pattern meets country industrial island: a concrete top, solid ash legs, and chromed collar supports combine with a modern Chippendale curved cupboard. Mixing history and iconic references makes for rich, unexpected variety and unique environments.

ABOVE 1930s style veneer construction. Pale directional aspen veneers set at 45 degrees and then composed in mirror patterned squares make a pleasant wood-covered surface that is easy on the eye.

ABOVE MIDDLE Evocations of historical styles connect you to another time and place. Here the use of bracket feet, fretwork patterns and breakfront construction are borrowed from eighteenth-century cabinetry pattern books.

ABOVE RIGHT Reinvention of traditional construction in this "Court cupboard" (my term for a grand cupboard.) This was a mispronunciation of "cours," or "short" from early French.

Most kitchens end up with a fair proportion of wood-fronted cabinets. With its huge variety and pattern, wood, in veneer form, offers the best grain configuration; with burls, quarter and roll sawn or ripple effects, the end results are far superior to using solid wood. The best and rarest trees are used for veneer cutting which, when combined with plywood or other suitable composite board, represent an ecological construction method for furniture.

Inlay is compatible, as it is cut at the same thickness. Large areas of veneer, without some kind of framework or proportion or grain change, can be dull, and lack the detail and scale suitable for furniture. It is practical in a kitchen because the surface is contiguous neighboring veneers, and therefore easy to clean.

For curved cabinets, inlay has the additional advantage of accentuating the shape, adding to the allure of its tiny components. There is a happy illusion that inlay is painstakingly put together in small pieces. Although made to high engineering standards of accuracy, it is sliced like bread from long lengths – not glued together, piece by piece. So it can be made in batch production quantities. Marquetry is the term applied to handcut pieces of wood veneer in either a pattern or picture, and has to be done by a craftsperson with artistic skills.

ABOVE Sourcing individuality. Handmade handles and copper nails to hold this clinker construction give originality to this island. Its double curve is complex and time-consuming to make.

RIGHT This hand-carved cabriole leg uses a sense of irony to create inerest and invocation of historical styles. The delicate carving sets the rough sawn finish of the column against the refined style associated with the Georgian period.

TOP Country-style herringbone inlay, typically made in oak and country woods. Inlay on this scale is more about pattern than the refinement or emphasis of line.

ABOVE A vertical tambour front in finely sectioned walnut invokes the 1930s and '50s, when it was used extensively – but it is practical to use space when door opening is constricted.

RIGHT A floor-to-ceiling wall-mounted grid cupboard with internal pierced aperture to a utility room beyond. Picture frame moldings present each of the cupboard doors as part of the canvas artwork, made of water-inspired patterns.

LEFT The pattern on this drawer front has a light and modernist quality that can be repeated in other parts of the kitchen to link the individual pieces of furniture.

ABOVE Glass panel fronts make the furniture appear lighter. The transparency can be an advantage, but it also forces you to keep the contents on show in perfect order.

LEFT Acid-washed glass bounces light back into the room and conceals any internal disorder rather well.

paint and pattern

The use of pattern and color offer good opportunities for personalization. Pattern is best used in small bands, intensively, particularly on key pieces at eye height. Why go to the trouble of doing a detailed piece of artwork if no one can see it? Many kitchens are constructed with copious quantities of wood, which can become soporific and light-absorbing in large quantities. Wood benefits from the contrast provided by painted surfaces and stone and metal textures.

We paint some cabinets in entirety for similar reasons. You can't normally apply such strong colors to a large area, but it certainly provides a welcome break with endless monotony of similar finishes. They are also easy to change when you tire of the color. Low-tech hand-painted surfaces are also easy to repaint if they get damaged. High-varnish polyester lacquers are affected by ultraviolet light and can't be matched if they get damaged. The judgment of an artist's eye to access light conditions in the room is a great asset, too.

LEFT A washed-out denim paint finish gives texture and, laced with a narrow ribbon of colored squares, produces a delicate pattern that works well in a modern interior.

BELOW The splashes of color in this tall kitchen are made up of various Russian Cossack-inspired patterns, both exotic and full of richness.

RIGHT Abstract patterns can break up large areas of wood cabinetry with dramatic effect; the colors chosen can complement the other materials, including floor surfaces. Here, a trio of abstract patterns within simple square panels – created using a denim style paint finish – complement the contemporary rubber flooring.

style and aesthetics **153**

storage racks

Racks planned as part of island design provide lighting gantries and an opportunity for hanging utensils within easy reach of the stove. Preferably they should be light and elegant in structure. Gantries are usually designed to a complementary shape and inset by 4 – 8 inches, to reduce the chance of making contact with the head. Lighting can play a prominent part, as a light source is more efficient closer to the work surface. On occasions when air extraction is required, the cover is softened by outriggers.

Useful for easy access storage and not just for decoration, plate racks are an efficient way of storing china and glassware. By using thin stainless vertical dividers, it is possible to fit in more plates per linear inch. It is possible to place racks in the center of a room as part of a subdividing wall, or they can be made convex and placed in corners.

TOP LEFT A hanging rack's primary role is as a lighting gantry. Here it is kept simple. Wood and metal in minimum sections echo the footprint of the island below. Without a gantry above, islands are less connected to architecture of the room.

LEFT This air extractor canopy, made of polished stainless steel and designed in a wedge shape to reflect the position and shape of the island below, is softened by outriggers.

ABOVE Using metalwork in places where you want strength and elegant structure together, as in this undercounter rack, makes for durability and complements the warmth of the wood against the cool and reflective qualities of the mirror-finished steel.

TOP Valuable multi-purpose wall storage in a narrow space is possible with careful detailing. Featured here are trays, display plates, a doweled rack for mugs and bowls, a narrow multi-purpose shelf for tableware and a blackboard for notes.

ABOVE This chunky wooden plate rack is ideal for a small kitchen. Teak dowels support the plates – the best wood to use where water is a constant presence.

RIGHT This plate rack design with thin vertical stainless rods saves space on using wooden dowels and creates a pleasing contrast with the surrounding wood. Cross dowels in the platform help locate the plates efficiently.

ABOVE Glass is becoming a more popular material within the kitchen framework. Here, toughened glass provides a chic countertop, while slumped and sculpted glass is used as a screen to partly conceal the cooktop from the table. The fridge panel, made from laminated, mirrored sculpted glass, creates unusual reflections.

RIGHT The shape, height and quality of work surfaces determine the activity. Here one area is for preparation, the other for serving.

FAR RIGHT Easily cleanable, durable surfaces are particularly important near a range. Mosaic is a flexible option as a wide range of colors and finishes offer an opportunity for subtle pattern.

OPPOSITE Slate on the walls and counters provides unity, practicality and a pleasant contrast where a lot of wood is present. End grain block, even on a small scale, indicates what to do and where. The design leads the function.

countertops

The choice of heights and materials of dedicated work areas is critical, not only in terms of durability and defining the practical purpose of each countertop, but also to add to the aesthetic quality of the whole space.

granite is an excellent starting point when considering durable and stain-free surfaces and is a sound choice for surrounding cooking areas where capacity for withstanding high temperature is required. Most granites have low porosity, but it is advisable to check.

slate and limestone are generally more porous than granite and have a more tactile and subtle grain. While new nontoxic silicone-based sealers are now available that make surfaces more stain-resistant, it is best to use the least porous types. Porosity can be tested by using a sample piece, apply oil or red wine and leave overnight. Alternatively, look at the density of a cut end and compare the weight with a similarly sized piece: the less holes and the heavier the sample means it is generally less porous. The same applies to limestone, which although softer than slate, comes in plenty of durable varieties suitable for use on secondary work surfaces.

marble needs more care than granite and is liable to damage from citric acid (e.g., from lemons) and red wine and, to a lesser extent, by oil. Providing any spills are cleaned up within a few hours, it will remain relatively unspoiled. Best used in secondary or tertiary positions, it is popular as a pastry or breadmaking surface. It must be well sealed first. You should also expect that it will become marked or pitted over time.

concrete is beneficial for its color control and thickness of worktop. It has a dry and pleasant light reflection, if mixed and finished well. It has a similar degree of porosity to slate but can be reduced by fine surface finishes and sealing.

stainless steel This is best used around wet areas such as the sink top. It can be made with seamless attachment to sink bowls, and the constant wiping means fingerprints don't become an issue, although it does scratch very easily.

wood Hardwood, with an application of an oil finish, is suitable for work surfaces. Chopping is best done on end grain as little damage is done to the surface where it is more dense. For areas where food will be prepared directly on the surface, use hot vegetable oil as a finish when it becomes dry to the touch. Do not use bleach. For other wood surfaces use Danish or teak oil to build up the thickness of finish you like.

floors

Selecting floor surfaces always involves a lively discussion and poses a difficult set of choices. The following comprise the most popular options:

wood The advantage of wood is its color, atmosphere and sense of familiarity, but in high-traffic areas, particularly around the sink, microscopic bits of dirt, aggravated by any moisture, react with shoe soles and can cause severe wear. There is a case for inserting separate materials, such as stone, rubber or terracotta there.

limestone Reflecting light back off the floor into the room is welcome, especially in dark rooms. It is best to avoid too clean a grain; fossil evidence and variety of color is more interesting, calming and durable.

terracotta Traditional terracotta tiles offer natural variation, textural interest and warmth. Whether reclaimed or new, choose from orange-pink or brown-red through to light brown colors. The best tiles are handmade, preferably wood fired – for both interest and safety. It is important to match the size of the tile to that of the room. Large rooms need bigger tiles to keep the overall effect fromo looking too busy.

ABOVE Large areas of wood need consideration to avoid soporific qualities affecting its enjoyment. Wooden floors mean that at least some pieces of furniture should have either painted facades or a high percentage of nonwood materials such as glass, stainless steel or mosaic, or have textural differences such as vertical ribbing, as pictured here.

RIGHT In heavy traffic areas, stone makes a more durable choice. Here the inside of a culinary circle is an appropriate point to make the transition from stone to wood.

OPPOSITE The area under the sink is the most demanding on floor use, as splashes of water frequently mix with dust and dirt. Here we used a rubber flooring – Dalsouple – to great advantage as it is both durable and soft under the feet.

LEFT Placing cupboards effectively means taking the space, position and function onboard together. A series of small cupboards around the window offer the bonus of a window seat. The floor-to-ceiling curved cupboard offers huge storage capacity.

BELOW Breaking up the levels of a fronted cupboard implies different storage in the top and lower sections – in this case, different categories of china.

RIGHT A mini kitchen built into the eaves of this timber framed barn. The circular table provides space for quiet reflection as well as space for eating a simple meal. The fold-back doors have open spoked panels that allow light through even when they are shut.

BELOW RIGHT Storage here is sequenced into a curved drum for china and table storage, while the tambour-fronted double appliance garage is used as an occasional work surface.

cupboards

Making the right choice of storage is key to a well-ordered kitchen:

curved corner cupboard Capacious and easy to access floor-based pantry. Using up corners in rooms where space is under pressure, the convex shape adds more storage capacity.

court cupboard Court cupboards provide layers of storage with the benefit of having a plinth to stand on to reach high-level storage. They can also house appliances, most commonly fridges.

grid cupboard Adaptable wall-mounted storage, good for narrow spaces. The grid cupboard comprises ordered segments that suit the storing of different items, from staple goods to cookbooks.

appliance garage Smart storage for small appliances, made with tambour fronts or fold-back doors. Appliances housed within can be permanently plugged in and used in situ on a good-quality work surface.

ABOVE Pivot drawer fronts are a good space-saving design when there is not enough depth for a proper drawer.

RIGHT Drawers with a corrugated wooden platform to take spice and herb bottles mean you can have them handy and visible. Most spices and herbs deteriorate if they are exposed to light.

RIGHT The front section of curved drums are usable – as shown here with a sub-divided drawer for flatware.

LEFT An angled wooden base in this drawer has varying widths to suit the size of each knife. This method of storage prevents damage to their cutting edges.

BELOW A deep drawer set in this chopping block provides useful storage for preparation utensils.

drawers

Different kinds of drawers offer you a chance to accommodate the size and accessibility of what you have to store. There is a general move to having more drawers in a kitchen since they can be used with less bending down and poking into dark corners. Drawers bring their contents out into the light. There are many configurations, as the examples on the following pages show. Our cabinetmakers create curved drawers to specific diameters, and solid wood is used in the construction. Plastic drawers tend to be made of vacuum castings that are weak and liable to rattle.

Special drawers conveniently accommodate spices when set up with a profile underneath to fit the bottles. Likewise for knives, although this has the disadvantage of being stuck with similar-sized knives in perpetuity. However, we usually design these profiles as drop-ins. Limitations with drawers are their front-to-back dimensions. Less than 10 inches usually means that mechanical drawer runners cannot be used and

ABOVE Tall and narrow pullout units are worthwhile, especially where, as in this barge, the width is only 4 feet and space is a constraint.

FAR RIGHT A horizontal pullout bottle rack is a good storage device in smaller kitchens where countertop space is reserved for practical tasks.

RIGHT A triple pullout storage unit above a work surface. Each one contains specific types of dry storage. The contents are immediately visible at a glance.

they fall out when opened. An excellent way of avoiding this is to use pivot fronts – but these only work if the drawers are relatively near eye level. You don't want to bend down to see inside.

Pullouts, or vertical drawers, are particularly convenient for narrow spaces, use up the leftovers of standard-sized cabinetry or simply provide a place to store the more awkward and smaller things that pile up in deep cupboards. An advantage of a pullout as pictured here is that all your small items are immediately on display at a glance. The taller items should be stored top and bottom, with heavy-duty drawer runners capable of holding considerable weights. It is advisable to work out loadings if you are going to store heavy pots and pans so that the right capacity drawer runner can be chosen when manufacturing the furniture. Although most of the examples illustrated on these pages show wooden interiors, various companies including Hafele, one of the biggest supplier of hardware to the kitchen trade, makes a huge variety of different kinds of metal pullouts that will cope with diverse needs of kitchen cabinet interiors, from ironing boards to pop-up work surfaces and double-depth pullouts. It is also worth giving thought to the right size of drawer handle. Big drawers need an easy-to-grip strong handle, while the case for small drawers, something more petite is suitable.

ABOVE LEFT
Drawers fill different uses, defined by their size. Handles need to be appropriate to the weight of the drawer when full.

ABOVE RIGHT
Curved end cupboards make an excellent place to store curved objects like plates or bowls as they fit snugly into the geometry.

LEFT Curved pullout trays hidden by drum doors. This is an imaginative use of complex craftsmanship and more luxurious than using metal.

appliances

Has technology really improved our cooking facilities? At the core of the "primal" kitchen we find three basic elements: fire, water and storage. The only real evolution that we find is in the appearance and technology. In the new school of thought, the belief is that the kitchen must be efficient to be productive. Technology certainly allows for more control and neater and safer cooking equipment, yet no amount of machinery can ultimately make for good cooking. That has to come from interest, accumulated knowledge, the desire to enjoy it and in the ingredients that make up your menu.

ABOVE LEFT Strong-grained marble in hues similar to stainless steel subtly offsets the impact that this professional-style range makes. The miniature wings provide extra parking space and safety from knocking pans off.

TOP An Aga provides great comfort as it is always on – effectively mimicking a hearth. It can fit sympathetically into a modern décor.

ABOVE Flat-fronted appliances can be made to fit in with curved cabinetry. Here the microwave is placed below countertop level.

ovens

Cooking devices should be chosen for ergonomic suitability. Each kitchen will benefit from at least one oven at high level, with a glass door for easy control of oven cooking and parking nearby, Lower ovens with a fold-down door provide a convenient place to check dishes that need to be returned to the oven. When choosing your cooking appliance, consider how often you cook and the method you prefer to use.

cooktops that have burners big enough for large pans and with a high BTU rating (the amount of heat capable of being produced) are vital for fast frying, wok cooking and boiling big pasta pots. Spacing of individual burners is important. If they are too close together, a group of pans won't fit on the cooktop.

grills The biggest gap in kitchen appliances relates to grilling. The inadequate infrared elements in ovens are problematic for many reasons. First, grilling generates a lot of fumes. It needs to be done fast and under constant supervision since food on the grill can burn easily. Next, it generates a lot of grease. You need serious ventilation for it, too. None of this is fulfilled in a conventional oven. Another disadvantate is that grease spills onto the sides of the oven walls, so the next time you use it as a conventional oven, the grease burns off, filling your kitchen with smoke.

ranges Professional-style cooking equipment, stoves and ranges of big proportions lend a prestigious note to any kitchen. They send out a message that a serious cook is around. They certainly are great for cooking on. I find ovens below get in the way when you are using the burners and prefer eye-level ovens. However, they are compact, they contain what are often dirty cooking activities within one area, and are robust in construction. North American ranges in particular have well-spaced gaps between the burners, and wider models allow two people to cook at the same time.

RIGHT Dual fuel burners are ideal for different types of cooking.Ceramic burners have the advantage of being usable for extra space when they are not in use.

TOP RIGHT It is crucial to plan appliances at the right height. An oven, microwave and dishwasher should be placed at convenient heights relative to their use.

agas have a different set of advantages. They are permanently switched on – the ovens, of varying temperatures, are ready and waiting. There is no need to wait for them to get up to the right heat, but they don't have as much precision in the temperature range as a conventional oven. They are reliable, well made using cast vitreous enameling, available in attractive colors and will last a lifetime. They make the kitchen warm in winter and – unless turned down to a minimum – hot in summer, which means they need backup cooktops and ovens, and they are very expensive. A lot of space ends up being devoted to cooking equipment. Agas need to be embraced by the architecture, either placed within an old chimney or framed in an architectural structure or casing.

A major technological achievement has been that quiet appliances are essential in the now predominantly social environment of the living room kitchen. Fridges, dishwashers and ventilation systems all have decibel ratings. Quiet appliances have made a major contribution to the kitchen becoming a sociable place, for how is conversation possible with noisy machinery?

microwaves

For reheating leftovers or defrosting, microwaves have their uses. Whenever possible, place them just below eye level so access is easy and sightlines uninterrupted. The disadvantage of a built-in microwave is that if it needs replacing you have to find one the same size. Many people now place them free-standing on a shelf inside a cupboard. This type costs less to buy, and the technology is no different from built-ins. It is important that the cupboard door should be either of a fold-back type or a tambour (like a rollup shutter) as constantly open cabinet doors in a busy kitchen thoroughfare is irritating. If you do house a microwave in a cupboard with hinged doors, make sure you provide ventilation as it produces odors and heat. Either way, don't forget to provide an electrical socket inside – cables don't look great poking out of cupboards.

dishwashers

Loading and unloading dishwashers involves around 120 actions, more than half in the lower drawer. This is slow work and bad for your back, especially if you are tall. We recommend avoiding this problem by raising their height by 14 inches wherever possible. It is also important to have the china storage cupboard immediately adjacent so that unloading can be carried out with economy of movement.

New options being offered by manufactures include hidden controls that are located on the inside edge of the lid. Although there are now many dishwashers being offered with a vast number of programs I think there is a virtue in purchasing those that have as little as possible to go wrong.

technological drawer Fisher and Paykel, a New Zealand company, have innovated a superb concept: dishwasher drawers. This allows you to load them without bending down as you do with standard height dishwashers. They can be installed parallel on either side of the sink, and can be run separately for cleaning up after small meals. This allows you to avoid installing raised height dishwashers in places where there is not enough room to have a high work surface in between the sink and storage points.

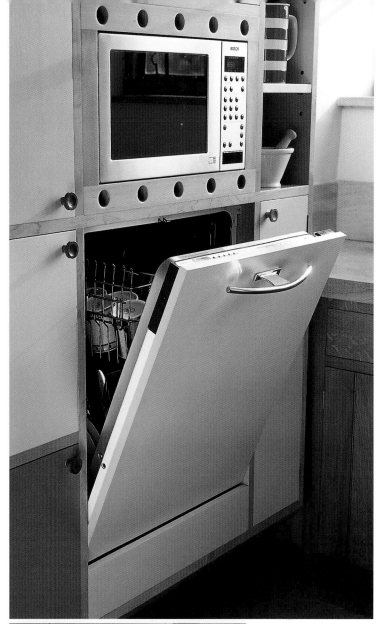

OPPOSITE Preparing and viewing. Here a TV is set back into a corner shelf within view of the table and preparation drum. In the cupboard on the right the built-in coffee-maker takes away the need to use valuable work surface as its platform.

ABOVE Raised height dishwasher. By taking it up 14 inches, the lower shelf can be reached without bending down.

LEFT Dishwasher drawers, invented by Fisher and Paykel. They are an excellent solution to avoid backbreaking stooping as they can be placed parallel on each side of the sink at a 36-inch height.

sinks

There are a lot of ways of tailoring the sink area to suit you personally. One large sink is better than two small, deep bowls – around 10 inches – as this prevents you from being splashed with dirty water. Bear in mind the height of the sink drainers should be set high because your working activity relates to the height of the bottom of the bowl. I prefer teak drainers because they are kind to fragile china that has to be hand washed and provide a quiet surface, but they need regular oiling and more careful consideration for water drainage. Stainless-steel countertops can be integrated with the bowls. A minimum of 24 inches is needed for draining surfaces on each side of the bowl, to accommodate normal washing up activities. To alleviate the boredom of washing dishes, wherever possible, place the sink in front of a window.

One of the most ergonomic designs we have developed is the use of a concave sink cabinet. A centerpoint is established in the middle of the preparation surface of the central island. From the edge of the cabinet we leave enough space for a person to work at each counter with some additional space to allow a third to walk through. The pedestrian flow is very smooth because the circumferences of the two work surfaces remain parallel. Distances are kept short, and the shapes are soft on the body and pleasing to the eye.

FAR LEFT TOP Integrated vegetable sink in a stainless steel quadrant. It is best to minimize wood around wet areas – with the exception of teak.

FAR LEFT BOTTOM Concrete double sink with sliding stainless steel drainer that also acts as a giant colander.

LEFT Curved stainless steel sink with deep basins and glass privacy screen.

ABOVE The convex plate rack complements the curved sink shape. It is backed by an acid-washed glass panel because it stands in the middle of a large space and therefore helps to keep the working area as bright as possible.

refrigerators

The best configuration for a fridge in spatial terms is wide and shallow. Easy access and storage for large items makes a 3-foot wide fridge ideal. Since the fridge is the second most used appliance in the kitchen, it is important that the main chamber be off the floor. As access between knee and shoulder height is the most convenient, putting fridges under a counter is a poor ergonomic choice. Fridges with deep-freezer drawers below make sense since the freezer is used less frequently, and the main chamber is likely to be at a convenient height.

There is much to be said for free-standing fridges as you don't have the expense of building cabinetry around them. And when you need to replace them, you don't have the tyranny of a specific size to fill. We also try to avoid stainless-steel fronted fridges as these need constant cleaning of fingerprints. Fisher and Paykel manufactures fridges with an iridium finish that looks like stainless but does not mark.

ABOVE Fridge drawers are handy in large spaces since they cut down on the amount of movement between key cullinary zones.

TOP RIGHT Dressing up the fridge as a piece of furniture. Big fridges can make quite an impact. It is not always appropriate, but here it fits well into the aesthetics of the room.

RIGHT A stainless steel free-standing fridge, such as this Sub-Zero model, has the advantage of being changed easily without any cabinetry work.

OPPOSITE TOP Coffee machines work well with some open space on each side.

OPPOSITE BOTTOM Warming drawers provide constant mid to low temperatures that some ovens cannot offer. It helps free the oven for other uses. Having two warming drawers means one can be used permanently for plates.

large fridges or small fridges The best configuration is a wide fridge, for example, 38 inches, with a shallow depth. Easy access and space for wide dishes is essential. Integrating large fridges like Sub Zeros provide a challenge. In our design studios we either leave them to stand alone in their stainless glory or frame them within a cabinet structure, subsuming them into a larger whole. Alternatively we use a decorative technique to humor them, for example, kilned and slumped glass with mirror backing. This clouds the glass surface so that fingerprints are not so obvious. A cold finish sits well on a fridge front. Stainless steel on the front of appliances is a cleaning hazard, since every fingerprint shows.

The position of fridges is best on the edge of the cooking area toward the direction of the table. If possible, because of the size of the door swing, keep the fridge away from the main preparation zone.

fridge drawers in large kitchens can be useful to cut down walking and can store everyday essentials that are easily reached for breakfast or light snacks, leaving the main fridge to accommodate bulkier raw ingredients.

cool rooms are an alternative for those who live in climates where heat causes food damage. There are a number of companies who specialize in providing the technology. The benefits are the dry, cold air that has lower moisture content than most fridges. This is helpful to extend the life of many foods. The most striking cool room we installed recently formed the inside of a free-standing circular cabinet. It was placed strategically between the preparation areas and the table.

two fridges that can be maintained at different temperatures is one option that some clients prefer. Lettuce, tomatoes and cheese are best if they are eaten straight out of normal fridge temperatures around $44° – 50°$ fahrenheit. Having a second fridge at $54° – 57°$ fahrenheit is useful.

coffee machines

The new variant for coffee machines is the built-in version. As with any built-in appliance, you are obliged to find a replacement of the same size. Although they make excellent coffee, I would be cautious about installing them. However, they have the advantage of taking away what is often a bulky machine from being placed on a worktop that is potentially useful for other more important tasks. Bear in mind they need plumbing in, and the electrics installed behind. The machine needs to be positioned at worktop level, and should ideally be adjacent to cupboards on either side that contain coffee, cups and other coffee-related equipment.

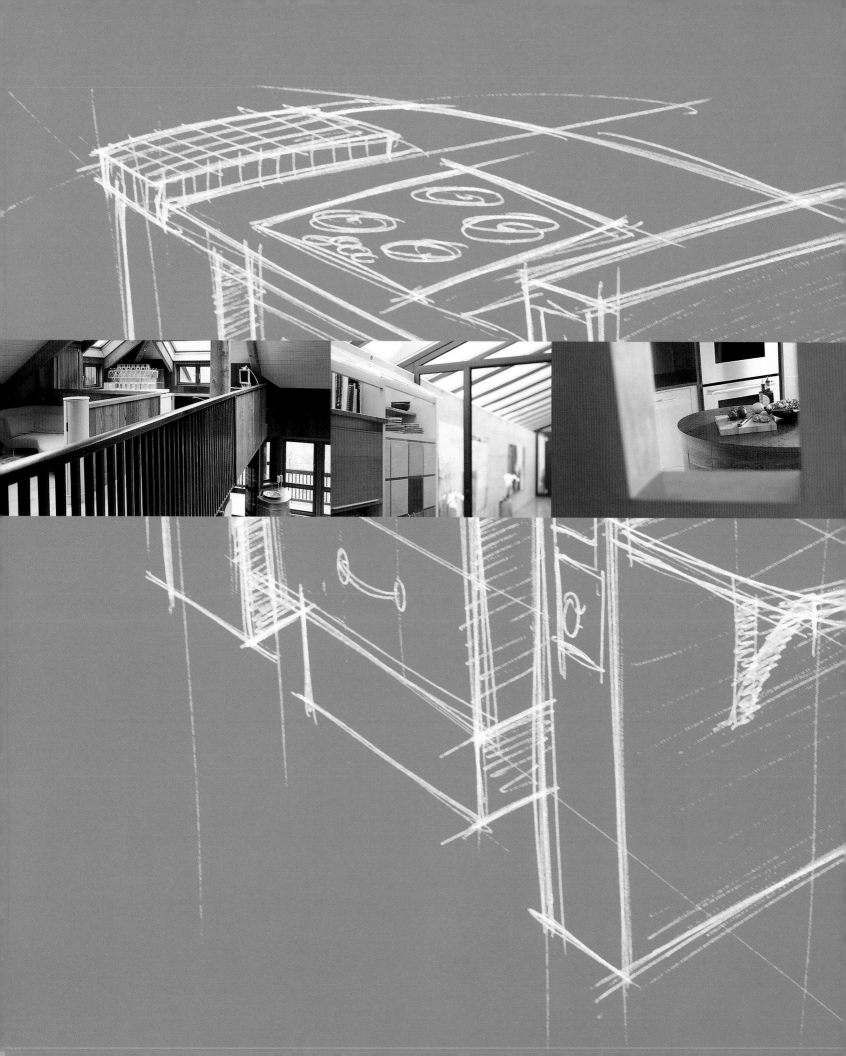

whole environment: architectural opportunities

No doubt kitchens, possibly more than any other room, reflect the personality of the owner. Well, mine is undoubtedly that of a clutter queen. It's a comfy mismatched kitchen that was furnished organically as we gradually acquired more possessions. There's a large old scrubbed kitchen table, a large Irish hutch, and a social sink that juts out across the kitchen, so I could chat to everyone as I cooked and washed the dishes. I now feel that the washing area should be somewhat obscured; masses of washing never looks sexy, no matter how delicious the food.

I've always hankered after a separate breakfast room, which was the tradition in my parents' and grandparents' house. A large window would face west to watch the evening sunset, with a windowseat where I could put my feet up and enjoy a quiet drink, or an outside porch as they have in Sweden.

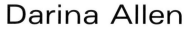

Darina Allen

defining a room

What is a room for? This a fundamental question to ask when you are thinking about redesigning or adapting your home. It is not enough to ask simply what use you intend for it. Rooms define not just the use of the space, but also your behavior in them; and they create useful boundaries for decoration. Changing the atmosphere of the various activity zones – using different floor and wall finishes, choosing original styles of furnishing and creating an intended atmosphere – are all part of the pleasure of creating a home. Understanding moods help make lighting and color schemes easier to establish.

vision beyond a familiar space

As the kitchen increasingly absorbs more active parts of downstairs life, analyzing the purpose and definition of a room, and understanding how to improve the architectural elements are vital because they help fit your lifestyle into the whole property more deeply. Ideas in this chapter are inspired by landscape architecture, such as view corridors and fully serviced environments; the whole interior needs to be right, from the furniture and floor textures, to the flow between rooms, and the lighting design. A well honed space filters the conditions of the day, allowing us to connect with nature and making us truly comfortable.

There is a necessity to mingle with natural light, good friends, and family for our personal well-being, and where better than in the new sociable kitchen where food and hospitality are at hand? The key requirements are: sufficient and efficient space, a high quality environment and an easy relationship to other rooms.

The current desire in an open kitchen is for a people-orientated active space. We all want to be part of household action – being in a thoroughfare that has zones of activity or rooms without walls is a fair description. An alternative model is a large hallway with areas for culinary activity, sitting around, eating, doing homework or just passing through, creating a more companionable environment, rather than dividing up these activities and spreading them around the house.

Last but not least is the residual use of small rooms to act as an antidote to the open-plan house – a quiet room where you can get away from it all. A place to withdraw is vital. Time spent contemplating, recovering from a busy day, collecting your thoughts or just having a quiet place to read a book is a good balance to aim for in planning the ideal kitchen.

planning for sociability

We need to make environments that support and complement the human mind and body in practical terms. The following ideas summarize the key aspects in making kitchens highly user-friendly and hard working.

- Main activities need to be carried out facing the center of the space, especially preparing food and cooking. The sociable part of cooking is the lead-up to the meal. Preparation gains a pleasant advantage through a glass of wine, music and chatting.
- Viewpoints in several directions promote social exchange. Eye to eye contact is desirable for conversation, so having multifaceted views is helpful in creating more sociability.
- A key "driving" position is something we try for in our kitchen spaces, akin to being in the driver's seat of a car. It is a spot where you can be in control. For example, the point in between the preparation and cooking area should be one of the best places for views of people within the room, to the entrance door and into the space. It should have a view of the outside of the house, particularly to see if visitors are arriving and, if possible, a view of the garden or landscape.

LEFT With the absence of walls between living and culinary areas, natural light evokes a warm, and inclusive environment that is conducive to sociable activity.

RIGHT The architecture of a room can make an essential contribution in helping to maximize the sociability of activities within the space.

- Distances are best kept to a minimum where active cooking is done. This allows for sociable areas to be closer and space for a sofa, café table or any item that is a semi-luxury beyond key cooking requirements. .
- Opt for quiet appliances, particularly extractor fans. Place fans inside the flue and not at the front surface near the cooking point, so they will make less noise. Quiet dishwashers and fridges are also important. And try to keep washing machines out of the kitchen. They are not designed to run quietly.

relaxed living

- Create a place to relax at the edge of the culinary zone. Soft areas with a carpet, couch or easy, lightweight chairs should ideally be outside a path and near a source of natural light.
- Using fireplaces as seating circles, cozy alcoves or sunlit areas for sociable activities increase their likelihood of attracting use since they have a clear sense of purpose.
- Comfortable perching places help to inspire short chat by offering unobtrusive places to sit or lean against. Many conversations are not planned. When we are in a hurry or in a domestic mood, most don't want the obligation of long conversations. Perching allows easy spur-of-the-moment chats to be possible without being awkward to end. The reverse side of the preparation area of the central island is a useful place for this, either as a raised breakfast bar or a low-level version akin to table height.
- Unusual places to sit or perch and objects to lean on provide a more relaxed version of the above but with a greater sense of transience.
- A second table or an area for children's homework is a practical idea in a large space since it means you don't have to clear the eating table after every meal.
- A desk for homework, computing or keeping household bills means you don't have to go to another room to do mundane, regular tasks.
- A staircase in the room enhances the amount of foot traffic through the space, particularly channeling people into the space from upstairs, and so making the room more of a hub.
- Include a comfortable telephone area where you can chat without being trampled on.
- Keep materials mixed throughout the kitchen. Create an interior mood through color, shape and a generally comfortable décor. Balance warm with cold, rich with light, old with new and most of all, make it feel cheerful.
- Ambient lighting with proper variation control systems are particularly important at nighttime so you can create dark areas to make the room feel cozier. Shadows create unknown areas around them that shrink the area visible to the eye. This helps create a calm and intimate sense of enclosure.

BELOW Creating drama through use of color and shape can transform a kitchen into a visual gallery and stimulating space.

OPPOSITE Free-standing furniture is very effective in drawing the eye beyond the immediate space, thereby creating a seamless connection beween different activity areas within an open-plan space.

space extensions

One of the main ways of making your kitchen bigger is by expanding the footprint of your property. If you think you have the opportunity, I have drawn up a checklist that you may find useful:

- After you have chosen the room or location for your kitchen and decided there is not enough space, look at the capacity of the yard for absorbing an extension, as well as the impact it will make on the house architecturally.
- Check the orientation. Where will the sun rise and what is the arc of sunlight you are likely to acquire? Will you be building a space in full sun or in shade? Both have advantages and disadvantages, depending on your climate. Too much sun can be just as much of a problem in a hot climate as being denied it in a cool one. Also consider the issues of wind exposure and proximity of trees. They can cause foundation problems, leaf clogging and dampness.
- Glass-dominated extensions can produce a substantial exposure to the elements. They become too hot in summer sun and inhospitable during drab winter days. We favor partial glass buildings, where at least some of the roof is solid and you cannot feel the upstairs stories hovering above you.
- Bringing the outdoors into the active kitchen can give you greater visual access as well as more light. Consider carefully where the best views will be and where to place windows to create view corridors – long-distance views or objects in the distance that help draw your eye out of the room and settle you in the landscape beyond. They create places where the eye will naturally rest.
- The architectural design of an extension falls into two camps, those which don't copy the style of the house and stand alone as a new piece of work, an expression of the time when they are being built – and those which try to blend in. If your extension falls into the former, a good way of thinking about it is to design it along the lines of a garden building with different materials from the main house. Its

differentiation makes it sit more comfortably as a more temporary lightweight structure.

- Formal extensions that will be incorporated into the property as if they were there from the beginning need serious integration and will be more expensive and complex, with careful copying of the house details and materials. If the extension is very small or there is an obvious way of filling in between two existing structures, this makes good sense.
- The problem with many extensions is that they look so obviously like add-ons. Buildings have character, and you can damage them by poor additions. To sensitive architects and lovers of old buildings, particularly old ones, there is a sense that they have manners too. Buildings respond to others nearby. Even though I think it is better not to fake it and try to overintegrate extensions, the issue remains that integrating new spaces is often hard to get right and the results can be awkward looking. One way to avoid this awkwardness is by making the addition as neutral as possible – a minimalist approach. This avoids a clash of architectural styles.
- New developments in glass technology creating the possibility of extensions made completely of glass. Double or triple glazing creates insulation standards that are the equivalent of double-cavity brick walls. By using small sections of high-tensile steel and toughened glass support pillars, you are able to design a glass box that has no other visible materials and is style-neutral. The transparency of the whole structure makes the result easy on the eye – it is hardly there.

removing walls

The classic way to make more space is to find it with the footprint of your existing walls. It is not always the easiest task or the one with the lowest cost, but sometimes there is space that is poorly utilized or an opportunity to break into a second room and make a fabulous large room.

- Begin by looking for redundant space in hallways. This is especially beneficial in semi-basements. It is often easy to find redundant space as our need for privacy has diminished and halls with a single purpose of connecting separate rooms are often unnecessary. If they are opened up, they often create access to a staircase, which is beneficial to an open-plan environment because it adds movement and sociability.

- The key dimension in a kitchen is the width of the room. If it is less than 15-feet wide there is not enough space for a central island, which is the most efficient configuration for a generous kitchen design. By removing a hallway an extra 4 feet may be found, allowing just enough space for an island to be incorporated into the kitchen plan.

- When breaking through to link two rooms into one, there is often the problem of exposed wall thickness – which, even when covered, looks raw, and there are often no equivalent architraves to use to make it look complete. This is where custom built pieces such as drum cupboards can be used effectively. They can wrap around the cut and provide storage, making up for the lost wall space.

- When making changes you will sometimes end up with tight, awkward or small spaces. With clever additions, even alcoves, bay windows and other imaginative architectural features, including places to sit or display sculpture or antique furniture, you can transform the use of the original room.

- An acid test for removing a wall is to ask the question: Does the house need the space you want to gobble up or will it make the room that is being augmented work more than 50 percent better? Does the house in question have at least one large room where you can entertain a decent number of people for special occasions? Do you want to have your children working and playing in a separate room when you are cooking a meal?

lighting design

There is a thirst for knowledge about lighting design because we now understand what a difference it makes. Indeed, lighting is not optional in a kitchen, it is a necessity. That is why it is vital to get it right. However, most homeowners don't have the expertise to do their own design, and bringing in lighting consultants and executing their ideas can prove expensive to implement unless you are refurbishing the whole space. Artificial light management in a northern climate means additional light is needed for much of the day as well as in the evening. Complementary lighting, different task lighting and the use of light as a way of defining rooms within rooms are vital to master in order to enjoy the space to its full advantage. At least four circuits are needed to complement the different functions – one each for working surfaces, façade boost, uplighting dining table use – plus any additional soft area requirements.

making the space work

- Work with natural light for daytime use. Plan key activities within the arc that the sun makes within the room, or in an area where there is a high level of daylight – near a window or skylight.

- Use the color scheme to provide brightness and light "bounce" that will increase the light level. Limestone floors and reflective walls in a dark spot can be helpful.
- Uncrowded furniture arrangements and space between or around them are helpful for creating a sense of spaciousness, which in turn makes for a clear and orderly space.
- Light all work surfaces in front of the body. Don't light from behind as the resulting shadows can be irritating.
- Use diffused light to soften aspects in the room and add interest. Diffused light is good for façades of furniture, or areas where you only want partial light.
- Directional light is useful where you want brightly lit areas.
- Create opportunity for different settings. Lighting control systems are as important as the light fixtures.

lighting control

The following comprise the main circuits needed in the average kitchen to make good use of the dedicated work ares and create the right mood:

the working circuit – a collection of lights on one switch for the key work surfaces. The light source needs to be between 48 – 55 inches from the surface for good-quality task light. In high-ceilinged rooms, bring the light source down from the ceiling on stems. It also makes the bulbs easier to change. The light source needs to be in front of your body to avoid shadows.

a secondary work circuit is for work surfaces or activities of lesser importance, and may include booster lamps for additional luminance.

a decorative circuit is useful for façade lighting of furniture, both for interior visibility and decorative interest on furniture. It can also be used generally to boost the light level when the kitchen is in high-action mode.

a separate table circuit is important because it means the light can be dimmed or turned off for use when candles are lit. This also allows you to control the light level of the working circuits independently.

an architectural feature circuit is designed to light the ceiling, fireplace or alcove feature. Typically, uplighters or hidden soffit lights are useful to create a dramatic effect.

RIGHT This unusual and effective use of glass as a transparent wall encourages natural light to fill the kitchen space and provide a contemporary mood.

OPPOSITE The use of floor-to-ceiling windows near the main cooking area makes the kitchen blend sympathetically with the outside, as it absorbs the natural light and shadows throughout the day.

LEFT Central islands usually need a hanging rack to help locate them properly. They serve as a lighting gantry and are an excellent way of bringing the task light onto the work surfaces.

OPPOSITE By night, a kitchen should exude warmth and atmosphere; this should be reflected in a flexible lighting arrangement.

general observations on lighting

- Light level either enhances or limits vision for the viewer. Objects recede in low-level light and come forward in bright light. Apart from becoming clearer, a bright area is more appropriate for handwork.
- Dim lighting prepares us for sleep, so it is considered restful. Hence we turn the dimmers down more as the evening progresses.
- Bright lighting allows for activity as it is linked to the circadian rhythms set by daylight.
- Varieties of light levels are necessary for perception of shape. Lighting rooms evenly is a failure if you want atmosphere.
- Reflectiveness of surface material indicates several possibilities; wood absorbs more light than paint or stainless steel. Too much reflection and you have eye burn. On large work surface, brushed stainless steel is preferable to shiny.
- Color vision needs bright conditions for its full color to be enjoyed; dark conditions lessen color impact. This may have implications for your choice of cabinet or wall colors.
- Warm/dark colors recede, cool/bright colors advance. In a narrow room, the long walls may be best muted and the short walls painted in a bright color to help reverse the hallway effect.
- In low brightness levels, blue-rich light sources offer more visual acuity (effectiveness) than yellow colors – almost triple the amount of perceived light.

lighting location

All rooms should have a series of set outlets at a low level for free-standing floor and table lamps – on a lighting circuit. They provide a flexible way of increasing light level and add a domestic atmosphere because they provide small, downward-pointing circles of light, creating intimacy.

Create the opportunity for different settings or use dimmer switches. Mount the control panel near the main doorway, by the table or both. Once you are seated at the table ready to eat you won't have to get up again to adjust the lighting.

light fixtures

- Downlighters set in the ceiling make for hidden low visual impact.
- Ceiling-mounted surface spots with swivel option offer good flexibility.
- Use track lighting for ease of installation (single connection) and flexible positioning. Low-voltage ones are best as they are a more discreet size.
- Rope lights comprise a low-voltage stainless steel cable that, when suspended from the ceiling or taken wall to wall, can be useful forflexible positioning.
- Undercabinet lighting is useful in dark areas below wall-mounted cupboards.

- Uplighters are excellent for bouncing light off ceilings. They produce a cold light, so should be planned as a secondary light circuit. They are also useful for adding extra illumination if you want more light evenly across the room.
- Drop rods are useful for tall ceilings where light would generally fall too wide for illuminating a specific target.
- Cantilevered lights from the top of furniture provide an opportunity to create dramatic shadows down the front. They also mean you do not have to try to hide cables.
- Floor lamps create downward light circles and are very flexible.

rules of thumb

- Establish visual hierarchy and focal points for key lighting "moments."
- For countertops, use approximately one lamp every 30 inches, except around the stove when it can be increased to one lamp every 12 inches.
- Avoid very shiny work surfaces with direct lighting above because the reflection is irritating and hard to work with.
- Dark countertop materials need more lighting as they absorb light.
- Don't overlight the culinary area in between key work surfaces because it overpowers that area of the room. It is pointless to light an area that is not in use.
- Leave dark patches in the room for the rest of the lighting to make an impact, especially around focal points.

bibliography

The Alexander Technique, Wilfred Barlow (Inner Traditions International,1991)

The Art of the Maker, Peter Dormer (Thames and Hudson, 1994)

Authenticity, David Boyle (HarperCollins, 2003)

Chez Panisse Café Cookbook, Alice Waters and the cooks of Chez Panisse, in
   collaboration with David Tanis and Fritz Streiff (HarperCollins, 1999)

Coming to Our Senses, Morris Berman (Unwin, 1990)

Concrete, Futong Cheng (Taunton Press, 2003)

Emotional Intelligence, Daniel Goleman (Bloomsbury, 2003)

Frank Gehry: Architect, Guggenheim Museum (Guggenheim Publications, 2001)

General Knowledge, Stephen Bayley (Booth Clibbon, 2001)

Hip Hotels, Herbert Ypma (Thames and Hudson, 2000)

Home, Witold Rybczynski (Penguin, 2001)

Is There a Nutmeg in the House?, Elizabeth David (Penguin, 2002)

Lighting by Design, Sally Storey (Pavilion, 2002)

Living on Thin Air, Charlie Leadbeater (Viking, 2003)

An Omelette and a Glass of Wine, Elizabeth David (Penguin, 2003)

The Rituals of Dinner, Margaret Visser (Penguin, 1991)

River Café Green, Rose Gray and Ruth Rogers (Ebury Press, 2000)

Taste: The Secret Meaning of Things, Stephen Bayley (Faber,1991)

Tomorrow's People, Susan Greenfield (Allen Lane, 2003)

The Twilight of American Culture, Morris Berman (Duckworth, 2001)

A Year at Ballymaloe, Darina Allen (Gill and Macmillan, 1998)

suppliers

countertops; stone and wood

Art Rock Creations Inc.
(Marble, granite and limestone fabrication)
602 McFarland 400 Drive
Alpharetta
Georgia 30004
T: 678 624-7763
www.artrockcreations.com

Belanger Laminates Inc.
(Manufacturer of countertop models
available in many colors and finishes)
1435 Joliot Curie
Boucherville
Quebec J4B 7M4
Canada
T: 450 449-3447
www.belanger-laminates.com

Buddy Rhodes
(Fabricates custom, integral color concrete
surfaces)
2130 Oakdale Avenue
San Francisco
California 94124
T: 415 641-8070

Cheng Design
(Designer and concrete artisan – works in
concrete to produce innovative concrete
surfaces)
2808 San Pablo Avenue
Berkeley
California 94702
T: 510 549-2805
www.chengdesign.com

DuPont Corian
DuPont Surfaces
CRP 721
4417 Lancaster Pike
Wilmington
Delaware 19805
T: 800 426-7426
www.corian.com

Formica Corp.
North America Product Design Group
10155 Reading Road
Cincinnati
Ohio 45241
T: 513 786-3400
www.formica.com

Fox Marble & Granite
(Offers a wide selection of stone and marble
countertops along with a state-of-the-art
fabrication facility)
1315 Armstrong Avenue
San Francisco
California 94124
T: 415 671-1149
www.fox-marble.com

Granite-Tops Inc.
12384 234th Street
Cold Spring
Minnesota 56320
T: 320 685-3005
www.granite-topsinc.com

Stone Solutions
2431 Los Berros Road, Bldg 2A
Arroyo Grande
California 93420
T: 800 547-5575
www.stone-solutions.com

tiles, glass and wall finishes

Corinthian Decorative Painting
(Specializes in a multitude of specialty wood
finishes, decorative plaster and gilding)
2443 Fillmore Street, #244
San Francisco
California 94115
T: 415 923-0500
Corinthian@world12.net

TBC Plaster Artisans
(Use traditional Italian materials in a
creative, urbane style associated with

contemporary Milan, including vibrantly
colored plaster finishes)
1045 Sansome
Suite 200A
San Francisco
California 94111
T: 415 362-3916

VillaFranca
(Specializes in decorative painting and
creative finishes for walls and surfaces as
well as commissioned fine art pieces)
2443 Fillmore Street, #186
San Francisco
California 94115
T: 415 626-4435

flooring

Armstrong
(Manufacturers of vinyl, linoleum, laminates
and hardwood flooring)
2500 Columbia Avenue
P.O. Box 3001
Lancaster
Pennsylvania 17604
T: 800 233-3823
www.armstrongfloors.com

First, Last & Always
("Floors as individual as you are")
P.O. Box 31776
San Francisco
California 94131
T: 415 753-8627
E: mail@first-last-always.com
www.first-last-always.com

Italy Home
(Suppliers of the finest in reclaimed antique
terracotta and stone flooring)
2 Henry Adams Street, #149
San Francisco
California 94103
T: 415 552-3063
www.italyhome.com

Pergo
(Manufacturers of laminate flooring)
P.O. Box 1775
Horsham
Pennsylvania 19044
T: 800 337-3746
www.pergo.com

Restoration Timber
508 San Anselmo Avenue, #9
San Anselmo
California 94960
Phone: 888 563-9663
E: info@restorationtimber.com
www.restorationtimber.com

Ann Sacks Tile & Stone
(Designer and distributor of a wide variety
of high-end stone tile and mosiacs)
8120 N.E. 33rd Drive
Portland
Oregon 97211
T: 800 278-8453 for store information
www.annsacks.com

Tony Kitz Gallery
(Specializes in antique carpets and textiles
of collector's quality)
2843 Clay Street
San Francisco
California 94115
T: 415 346-2100

Walker Zanger
(Manufacturer of high-end stone, ceramic,
metal and glass tile)
8901 Bradley Avenue
Sun Valley
California 91352
T: 713 300-2940 for store information
www.walkerzanger.com

lighting equipment

Glasslight Studio
(Custom lighting composed of hand blown or
fused glass finished in a variety of hardware
options for wall, ceiling or table)
T: 610 469-9066
E: glasslyte@aol.com
www.glasslightstudio.com

Kichler Lighting
(Decorative light fixtures, lamps and
accessories)
7711 East Pleasant Valley Road
P.O. Box 318010
Cleveland
Ohio 44131-8010
T: 800 875-4261
www.kichler.com

TC Electric
(Specializes in both residential and
commercial projects. Certified for Lutron
Homeworks and Radio RA installation and
programming.)
2 Henry Adams Street M-42
San Francisco
California 94103
T: 415 431-2699
E: mitch@tc-electric.com
E: Jamie@tc-electric.com
www.tc-electric.com

lightspace design

Architectural Lighting Design
13 Aglipay Drive
Amherst
New Hampshire 03031-2131
T: 603 886-4636
E: sfrenette@lgtspace.com

media equipment and control systems

Kashyk Designs
(Supplier and installer of custom designed
sound and media equipment)
T: 510 522-6008
www.kashyk.com

soft furnishings

Lisa Staprans Interior Design
(Celebrated interior designer Lisa Staprans
has collaborated with Johnny Grey for many
years, including our San Francisco
showroom. She also works directly with the
artisans and craftspeople who make up the
Grey Guild.)
159 Ramona Road
Portola Valley
California 94028
T: 650 851-8436
E: lisa@stapransdesign.com
www.stapransdesign.com

appliances

Amana
(Major appliances, including refrigerators,
freezers, dishwashers, wall ovens, ranges,
cooktops and microwave ovens)
403 W 4th St N
Newton
Iowa 50208
T: 800 843-0304
www.amana.com

Electrolux Home Products North America
(Powered appliances for the kitchen)
6150 McLaughlin Road
Mississauga
Ontario L5R 4C2
Canada
T: 800 668-4606
www.electrolux.com

Fisher Paykel
(Suppliers of high-end appliances for the modern-day home)
T: 1-888-936-7872
E: usa@fisherpaykel.com

KitchenAid
(Manufacturer of state-of-the-art dishwashers and professional quality cooktops, refrigerators, stand mixers, cookware and more)
P.O. Box 218
St. Joseph
Michigan 49085
T: 800 422-1230
www.kitchenaid.com

Kuppersbusch USA
4920 W. Cypress Street, #106
Tampa
Florida 33607
T: 813 288-8890
www.kuppersbuschusa.com

Sub-Zero Freezer Co.
(Manufacturer of Sub-Zero refrigerators, freezers and wine storage units)
P.O. Box 44130
Madison
Wisconsin 53744-4130
T: 800 222-7820
www.subzero.com

Thermador
(Manufacturer of gas and electric cooktops, ovens, ranges, ventilation, dishwashers and barbecues)
5551 McFadden
Huntingdon Beach
California 92649
T: 800 656-9226
www.thermador.com

specialty sculptural elements

Redhouse Studio
(An innovative design-built sculpture studio specializing in custom cast and fabricated metal architectural statements)
518 South Arthur Avenue
Pocatello
Idaho 83204
T: 208 478-0269

Metalurges
(A fabricator of custom metalwork, primarily using stainless steel, copper, aluminum, brass and zinc, in addition to a multitude of finishes and patinas to create unique pieces)
124 Delabarre Avenue
Conway
Massachusetts 01341
T: 413 369-4451
E: metalurges@rcn.com

cooking and kitchen equipment

Bed, Bath & Beyond
650 Liberty Avenue
Union, New Jersey
T: 800 462-3966 for store information
www.bedbath.com

Crate & Barrel
1860 West Jefferson Avenue
Naperville
Illinois 60540
T: 800 967-6696 for store information
www.crateandbarrel.com

Sur La Table
1765 Sixth Avenue South
Seattle
Washington 98134
T: 800 243-0852 for store information
www.surlatable.com

The Terence Conran Shop
407 East 59th Street
New York
T: 212 755-9079
www.conran.com

Williams-Sonoma Inc.
3250 van Ness Avenue
San Francisco
California 94109
T: 800 840-2591 for store information
www.williams-sonoma.com

kitchenwares

Canadel Furniture
(Kitchen furniture)
700 Avenue Canadel
Louiseville
Quebec J5V 2L6
Canada
T: 819 228-8471
www.canadel.ca

Fishs Eddy
(Vintage and new kitchenware)
889 Broadway
New York
New York 10003
T: 877 347-4722
www.fishseddy.com

Hammacher Schlemmer
(Unique housewares)
147 East 57th Street
New York
New York 10022
T: 800 421-9002
www.hammacher.com

Villeroy & Boch Tableware Ltd
(Classic or modern, formal or casual, tableware from Europe)
5 Vaughn Drive, #303
Princeton
New Jersey 08540
T: 609 734-4800
www.villeroy-boch.com

index

acknowledgments

I owe the opportunity to publish this work to the patronage and generosity of my clients who have trusted in my company and my craftsmen to carry out the work in often arduous and demanding circumstances. Without their support and agreement to return for a second round of interruptions with our team of photographers, this book would not have been possible. In no particular order, I would like to heartily thank the many wonderful clients I have worked for, especially the ones whose projects appear in this book. They are Marian and Arthur De Curtains, Marian and Carl Presig, Barbara and Arthur Macmillan, Jane and David Gault, Loretta Tomasi and Paul Middlemass, Pamela and Aubert De Villaine, Alison and Tony Purnell, Felix Dennis, Sarah and Tim Bunting, Caroline and Graeme Finnie, Pam and Keiran Murphy, Andre and Caroline Vrona, Andrew Solomon, Graham Bond, Jeanette and Simon Nelson, Karen and Ian Landy, Harriet and Jake Macfadden, Evi and Michael Kaplanis, Pam and Peter Forrester, Tamlyn and Rupert Harrison and Emma Blackburn and Don Gallis.

I am hugely grateful for the hard work of the studio team I have had around for the last 10 years. My sincere thanks to my stalwart visual artist, Richard Lee, who has consistently produced artwork illustrating our designs for over 10 years in a mouthwatering fashion that makes me want them as much as the clients. My thanks to Anna Moore, my recently departed loyal administrator and guide, and to Nicki Arnold, our current administrator. A big hand of gratitude for Ethan Maynard, who ran the studio for six years in such a gemütlich way, Mike Rooke for his good taste and contribution on several levels, from design through to site work, Juliet Carr for her elegant design and personal skills, Clare Devlin for her talented design work and Daryl Debbage for his practical skills. My current team deserves a fair mention, too: Tina Wheeler, my dedicated and hardworking UK design studio manager, Miles Hartwell, my inspired UK creative director and Matt Whithington, my talented UK designer and provider of the stylish sketch drawings that pervade the pages of this book and give a cogent representation of how we develop our designs.

In the USA studio I want to acknowledge particularly the commitment and vision of our energetic CEO, Peg Bausch, our superb new design principal, Kevin Hackett, and Caroline Nichols, our showroom manager.

Our craftspeople deserve the greatest praise for their skill and hard work. Three individuals and their co-workers who have helped me enormously over the years are Jonathan Morris, Nigel Brown and Alistair Black. Woodworkers of the highest talent include Steve Cordell and John Parlet. Some wonderful installers, including Andrew Parslow, artists, architects, builders, metalworkers and painters have all made huge contributions. I would like to thank Lucy Turner, Felicitas Aga artists in their own right whose skill with paint and pattern is so outstanding.

I would also like to thank those who have made this book possible. Special thanks to Jaqui Small, my publisher, who had the bravery to commission the book in the first place. Kate John, my editor has kept the project on the road and done a hardworking job putting my text in order, refining where necessary and turning it into a wholesome book. My gratitude to Alex Wilson and his assistant Sarah Hogan for their extraordinarily beautiful photography. Alex managed to produce poetic natural light where there was little more than a modicum of evidence of it and turn our interiors and details into images rich in atmosphere and visual delight. And many thanks to designer Maggie Town for her creative artistry.

I must acknowledge special thanks for the constant, uncomplaining support of my long-suffering wife, who must be forgiven in thinking that my laptop was a third party in our bedroom for the duration. To my children, Harry, Felix, Gussie and Benny, who put up with me being distracted weekend after weekend, when I would have been a better Dad by spending time with them. They never gave me a hard time and always were keen for me to complete the book to high standards.

Lastly, please forgive me, those whom I have failed to mention. So many individuals from all walks of life have made our work possible. All building and design projects only work when there is collaboration.

All photographs are by Alex Wilson except for those taken by Jason Lowe (p10, 3rd from left; p14, p15, p17 bottom left and right; p18, p23 and p24; Francesca Yorke (p13 and p19), courtesy Johnny Grey; David Helsby (p51, top), courtesy Johnny Grey; Trevor Richards (p130, bottom; p135, bottom; p148, p179, p183), courtesy Johnny Grey; Matt Millman (p166, p170, bottom), courtesy Johnny Grey; Andrew Wood p170-1, main picture.

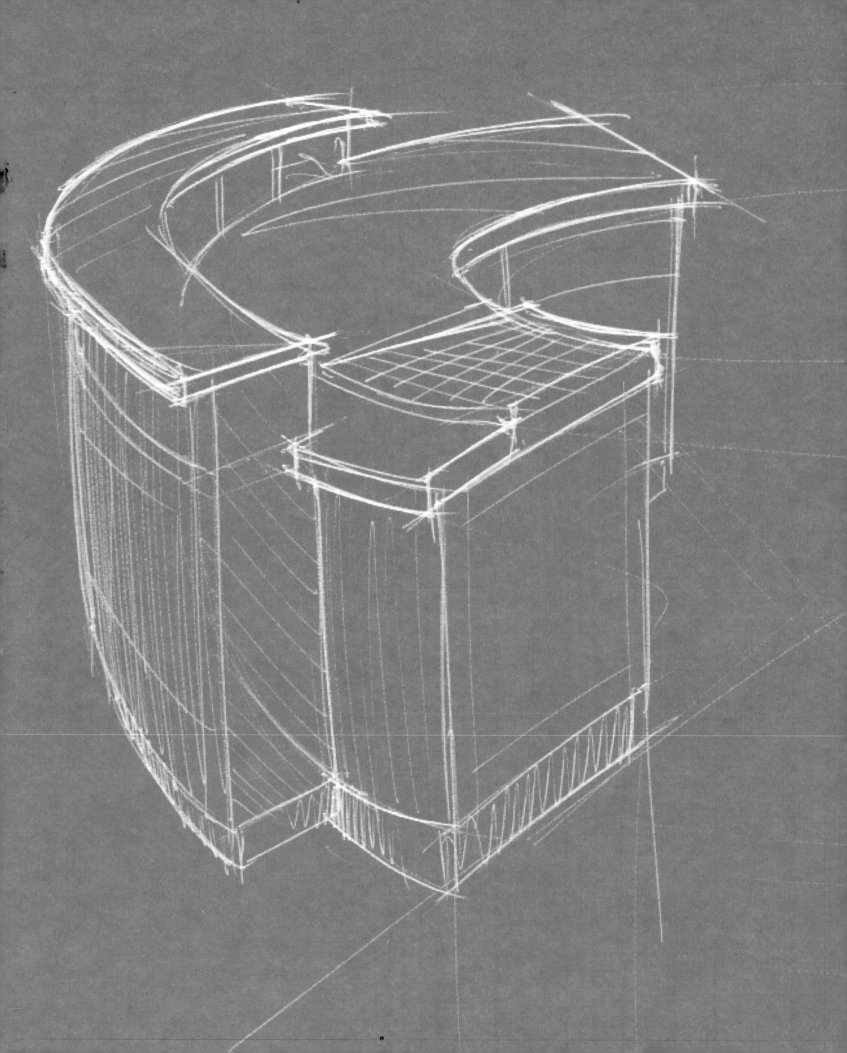